Chatham House Papers · 26

South Africa 1984

A plume of smoke issued daily from the mouth of the volcano above the villagers below, who continued to tend their vines without thought of the morrow.

(Bulwer Lytton, *The Last Days of Pompeii*)

People crushed by laws have no hope but from power. If laws are their enemies, they will be enemies to law; and those who have much to hope and nothing to lose will always be dangerous more or less.

(Edmund Burke, Letter to Charles James Fox, 8 October 1777)

Chatham House Papers · 26

South Africa 1984

Dennis Austin

The Royal Institute of International Affairs

Routledge & Kegan Paul
London, Boston and Henley

First published 1985
by Routledge & Kegan Paul Ltd
14 Leicester Square, London WC2H 7PH
9 Park Street, Boston, Mass. 02108, USA and
Broadway House, Newtown Road,
Henley-on-Thames, Oxon RG9 1EN
Set by Hope Services, Abingdon and
printed in Great Britain by
Billing & Son Ltd, Worcester

ISBN   0-7102-0620-8

Contents

Glossary

There is often a Humpty-Dumpty air about words in South Africa: they mean whatever is ascribed to them. A national state, for example, is one in which a majority of that state's nationals do not actually reside. An independent republic under tribal rule is an area (or several disjointed areas) wholly dependent on South Africa. 'White South Africa' is mainly black. Asians are frequently referred to as Indians. Coloureds are people of mixed race — the unclaimed progeny of Afrikaner loins — and include many shades of colour from near-white to near-black. To help understanding, therefore, the following short glossary is appended.

Apartheid Literally 'separateness', a chameleon word that often changes its meaning and skin, though only within a modest range of colours.

Africans 22 million (c. 70% of pop.). The 1980 official census gives 17 million, since it excludes the populations of Transkei, Bophuthatswana and Venda (*see* 'Independent republics'). Main divisions: Xhosa, Zulu, Swazi, Ndebele, Sotho, Tswana, Shangaan.

Asians 1980 census: 821,320 (c.3.2% of pop.), including some 11,000 Chinese. About 85% live in Natal, most of them within 100 miles of Durban. Divided linguistically between Hindu (Tamil, Telugu, Hindi, Gujurati) and Muslim (Urdu).

Coloureds 1980 census: 2,612,780 (c. 10.5% of pop.). Imprecisely defined but including Griquas and the Muslim Cape Malays. About 85% live in the Cape Peninsula.

Whites 1980 census: 4,538,000 (c. 17% of pop.). A mixed group: Afrikaners (60%), English-speaking (40%), Jews 120,000, Portuguese 57,800, Germans, 40,240, Greeks 17,000.

RSA Republic of South Africa — the area governed under the 1983 constitution, which excludes the independent republics.

Independent states The four homelands which opted for independence: Transkei (1976), Bophuthatswana (1977), Venda (1979), Ciskei (1981).

Self-governing homelands   Self-governing, but not independent, homelands Lebowa, Qwaqwa, KwaZulu, KwaNdebele, KaNgwane, Gazankulu.

Southern Africa   The sub-continent, including all the above, plus Lesotho, Swaziland, Botswana, the neighbouring republics of Mozambique, Zimbabwe, Angola, Namibia, Malawi and lands across the Zambezi.

ANC   African National Congress, originally brought together in 1912.

AZAPO   Azanian People's Organization (1978), heirs of the Black Consciousness movement and its Black People's Convention.

Frelimo   Front for the Liberation of Mozambique.

MPLA   Popular Movement for the Liberation of Angola.

PAC   Pan-Africanist Congress — a radical breakaway movement that separated from the ANC in 1959.

SADCC   Southern African Development Coordination Conference — formed in 1980 by leaders of the African 'front-line states' to try to strengthen economic ties among themselves.

SWAPO   South West African People's Organization, Namibia.

UDF   United Democratic Front (1983), a multiracial alliance of opposition to apartheid.

UNITA   National Movement for the Total Liberation of Angola.

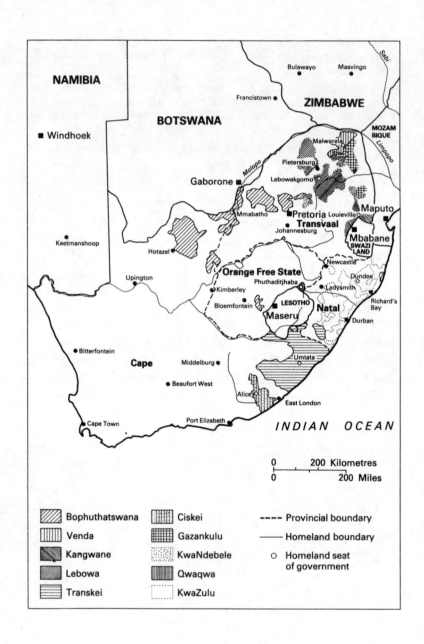

Republic of South Africa, including national states

1 Introduction

The question examined in this essay is whether South Africa can fill the gap left by the withdrawal of colonial power from southern Africa or whether it will itself become a battlefield. It is the central problem in the familiar puzzle about National Party rule, whether it can truly change in order to survive. 'A state without the means of some change', said Burke, 'is without the means of its conservation.' But how much change is required of South Africa if it is to ensure its preservation? It is in the nature of such questions that no clear answers are possible, yet they lie at the heart of a second problem discussed in these pages: namely, what is a sensible policy for Britain and its Western allies to adopt in their relations with Pretoria? Should they do something, or nothing, to try to influence the course of events in the large region of southern Africa?

The material presented to the reader for judgment is not conclusive. How could it be? There can be no assurance about future events. At the end of 1984, when this paper was written, South Africa was a major regional power, but the government needed the full force of the state to curb non-white protest. There was uncertainty, too, over the disjunction between economic forces calling for change, and political fears which confirmed existing structures of power. Meanwhile, Britain and other Western governments, while continuing to criticize apartheid, based their relations with the Republic on the hesitant assumption that the National Party government, though unpleasant, was not unstable: repression seemed likely to be equal to revolt.

In fairness to South Africa, such a view was not the picture painted by officials in Pretoria. They insisted that change was on its way, and that the dismantling of apartheid was certainly a possibility. It would not, they said, happen overnight. Nor would South Africa surrender to

1

black rule, but changes were on their way which would ensure the future of the country, not through repression, but through reform. Mr P. W. Botha, prime minister after 1978 and now president, had promised as much and there was ample evidence to support him.

The claim is worth testing. South Africa has always been a land of fantasy, given over to deception: the country based on gold has been an easy prey to illusion – a Midas state grown rich by the fable of gold. What else is apartheid but a belief in the illusion of separation? But perhaps the justification of European control is beginning to yield to more plausible dicta than the dogma of race: of white is right? In effect, there has been a frustrating paradox about arguments for change in South Africa – the white minority being prepared to endorse reform in order to remain the same, non-whites demanding change in order to bring about reform. Has that paradox been resolved? There is a different constitution now, and new legislation based on commissions of inquiry. There is said to be a growing African middle class. Coloureds and Indians have the vote. Proof of the earnestness of these reforms, it is argued, can be seen in the difficulties facing the ruling National Party. There have been denunciations of government policy by those who had been stalwart supporters. That, too, is worth examination. Since revolutions begin when rulers fall out, one ought to try to measure the strength of Afrikaner discontent.

It is certainly worth recalling how shaken white South Africa was at the end of the 1970s. There had been a series of misfortunes: the flight of Portugal from Mozambique and Angola, the end of settler rule in Rhodesia, the growing strength of SWAPO, an international arms embargo, the slackening of American support, the advance of Soviet interests (Cubans in Angola and Russians behind the Cubans), the rise of a Black Consciousness movement in the Republic and the ugly events of 1976 in Soweto. South Africa had been at bay, flanked by its enemies and facing disturbances at home. The strength of P. W. Botha lay in devising a total strategy to combat what appeared to be a total onslaught. He had brought the defence forces up to scratch, equipped them with modern, locally produced weapons, tested them in combat and thereby reassured the white electorate that South Africa could survive attacks upon it. It was the reasoning behind armed incursions into Angola, Mozambique and Lesotho, and of a harsh diplomacy towards Mugabe in Zimbabwe. South Africa had had to stand alone, and the National Government in Pretoria succeeded in demonstrating its power to hurt.

Later came the turn from destabilization to domestic reform and regional détente. The most telling evidence was said to be the 1983 constitution, the recognition of black trade unions, the easing of restrictions on the employment of labour and a recognition of the need to examine the problem of black political rights within the Republic. Abroad, the most conspicuous achievement was the March 1984 Nkomati Accords with Mozambique. A treaty had actually been concluded with Marxist enemies across the border. Similar agreements were being sought with South Africa's other neighbours, Namibia was being argued over rather than fought over, and the United States — along with its Western allies — had drawn closer to events in southern Africa as a whole.

It was on the basis of these claims of reform at home, success abroad, that Mr Botha ventured overseas in June 1984 to seek the approval of Western governments. He was received rather distantly, but the visit itself was offered as proof within South Africa of his skill. In the early 1980s, therefore, the government claimed to stand more confidently on its authority, not as the architect of repression, but as the initiator of change. Reform at home and peace abroad, it was argued, would bring stability and prosperity to a region in a continent which had known little of either. In effect, the pariah was rejecting his outcast state and asking for sympathetic consideration.

The claim by Pretoria to be in managerial control, backed by the promise of change, transmits signals that the West is inclined to receive. After all, reform is more likely to be born of stability than of disorder. And the case made out is not implausible — a new constitution, a relaxation of racial laws, economic growth, social progress and a movement towards a less doctrinal form of apartheid. Perhaps it is true that white South Africa has the capacity to reform and has by no means exhausted its ability to change? Why not, therefore, give Pretoria some measure of credence and some allowance of time? Admittedly, violence within the African townships persists; it seems that it cannot be eradicated. But — runs the argument — very likely it can be contained, as in other parts of the world. Britain has learned to live with Ulster; the United States worked its way through ghetto disturbances. South Africa, too, ought to be able to smother dissident movements and pen back the violence of Sharpeville and Soweto. There is, to be realistic, an 'acceptable level' of urban terror in many modern societies — acceptable in the sense that, however horrible such outbreaks may be, they do not greatly disturb the daily busy life of a developed, industrial society.

The argument is familiar and attractive to Western governments, since, if it can be sustained, it may be possible — now, in the mid-1980s — to push the question of South Africa further down the list of the world's problems than had once seemed likely. It will still be a problem, but it will not be an immediate problem. After all, the world is full of wrongdoing, and South Africa is one of many oppressive regimes. It is also a sullen world of little idealism at the present time. A good deal has gone sour. During the 1960s, Western governments still believed in the management of a set of international relationships which since 1945 had included states they had nursed into adulthood. The hope was of representative government and civil liberties, and although many of the post-colonial countries did not care for their origins, they too trusted in a nationalism which would underpin democracy and an independence which would promote development.

There are few such hopes today. There is an endangered world of nuclear terror and a long catalogue of oppressors, among whom black African governments are prominent, in Ethiopia, Uganda, Zaire, Sierra Leone, Liberia, Sudan, Nigeria — the list grows daily longer, and the mood among Western governments has changed. It is more sombre, less idealistic, and places a premium on stability and control. South Africa seeks to offer both. It rules with a heavy hand at home and dominates a substantial area of a continent full of unrest. It is positioned strategically at the southern juncture of the Indian and Atlantic Oceans, possesses enormous mineral wealth, sustains a large volume of trade with the West, and claims cousinship — however many times removed — with West European society. Why should it not be accepted as a familiar, if disagreeable, member of the international community on the same footing as other areas of the world whose governments are sometimes friendly, sometimes hostile, to Western interests?

In a sense, all these questions are one question: is South Africa stable and is it capable of change? The concluding chapter goes some way to attempting an answer, but the reader should not look for more than limited guidance through the uncertainties that characterize South African society. We like to believe that there are 'ascertainable facts' as evidence of what may come, but the facts themselves are usually shaped by one's own predilections, and arguments about the likely fate of southern Africa are rarely more than fragments of a mosaic which men shape to suit their fancy. There is also a tendency in the literature on apartheid — the writer is not wholly innocent in this respect — to go on tap-tapping the dry rock of statistics in the hope of releasing a fresh stream of information about the future; but there is little profit in it. There are no Markov chains of probability of revolution. Nor are the politics of men like the mechanics of celestial bodies. Indeed, one is tempted to add that, for white South Africa, it is not the future but the past which is unpredictable; for how is one to interpret the history of the National Party, whose leaders not only systematized apartheid but believed it to be a workable framework for an industrial society?

Better, therefore, to present the reader with a snapshot of the Republic as it appeared to the author in the last months of 1984 — a camera's eye which also uses the past to try to explain the present. Explanation rather than prediction. In the gentle art of what biblical scholars know as hermeneutics, interpretation and explanation have been invaluable for study of the scriptures, and it is to be hoped that they can provide a sensible mode of inquiry even into so ungodly a country as South Africa.

2 Domestic order

Theory before fact. As one talks to government spokesmen, and reads the carefully presented *Official Yearbook of the Republic of South Africa*, issued by the Department of Information, a picture emerges of a controlled and manageable society—manageable, that is, in the eyes of National Party leaders. It is a portrait of the Republic under a president who wishes to impose his own stamp of authority on the peculiar society that is South Africa. It is, in fact, so strange a country that the gap between reality and theory is wide, and theory has to be enlarged from time to time. The 1980s, the decade of Botha, are a modification therefore of the 1960s, the era of Dr Verwoerd and his successor, John Vorster. So strong was the impress of Verwoerd, and so out of keeping were his policies with the passage of events, that by the middle of the 1970s change was inescapable. Not only the way in which society was governed, but also the theory by which it was defended, called for reform. President Botha versus Dr Verwoerd, the 1980s against the 1960s? That would be a crude way of expressing what has happened, but crudeness has its advantages and it is with the contrast between doctrinal apartheid in the 1960s and modified apartheid in the 1980s that one may usefully begin.

Common to both periods has been the notion of South Africa as a plural society of white, black, coloured and Indian communities — that familiar vocabulary of colour — who, because they are culturally distinct, ought (it is said) to be politically separate. The distinctive feature of the 1960s was the attempt to present South Africa as being divided not hierarchically — whites on top, blacks underneath — but geographically, the white Republic and black homelands. The argument ran as follows. Britain was beginning to grant independence to Lesotho, Botswana and Swaziland. South Africa would give self-government to its own natives.

There would be national states of Zulu, Shangaan, Xhosa, Sotho, Tswana, Venda — tribal identities under traditional leaders. If a local word were needed, they might be described as Bantustans (native areas): the underlying principle would be, not baasskap (boss rule), an outmoded concept, but political separation within the single economy of southern Africa. Europe had distinct nationalities within a common market. South Africa would follow suit. There was already a customs union of the soon-to-be-sovereign states of the region: why should their number not be added to?

It was on the basis of such arguments that relations between white and black were raised to a new height of theory, almost an ideology. It was the man from outside, Hendrik Verwoerd, Dutch-born and bemused by theories of psychology and race, who provided the justification of policies that were to dominate the 1960s. Behind the policies lay the claim to morality. And it was the 'morality' of apartheid that dragged South Africa further down the road towards a totalitarian society under an imposed pattern of beliefs.[1] In moving in this direction, Verwoerd did South Africa perhaps the greatest disservice it was possible to inflict on a country that was already becoming isolated. He gave the policy of white control a name that was seized on by the outside world as the epitome of man's inhumanity to man: apartheid. A moral gift to the righteous and a mirror in which Western man has seen himself reflected very uneasily. Apartheid theory gave form to racial categories, gave them degrees of subordination in the scheme white/coloured/Indian/black. The classification was meticulously expressed in law and brutally enforced by magistrates and police.

For a time, this answered white needs. Although the National Party achieved republican status for the country in May 1961 (at the same time seizing the opportunity to quit the Commonwealth), the Republic was not fully established. Memories of the 1930s still survived, of poor whites and English domination. Job reservation under apartheid laws gave the urban worker from the platteland the economic protection he needed; the Group Areas Act enabled him to sleep secure in his whites-only towns and suburbs. When one looks back from the 1980s, it is possible to note the extremism of the Verwoerd years. It was too dogmatic, say critics today, too rigid, too *verkrampte*, too extreme a version of earlier policies under Hertzog and Malan. Very likely that was so, although a belief in racial separation runs like a thread through the full history of Afrikaner nationalism, from the early years of the Het Volk party and the Broederbond to that dour achievement of the National Party which fashioned the 1961 republic in the image of its predecessors.

Apartheid worked. Nor is it difficult to see its effects today. Drive out from Bloemfontein in the Free State, and the road stretches emptily into the karoo: 600 kilometres between breakfast and supper is an easy run. The pattern of control between white and black is well illustrated by the little towns scattered across the veld. The road stretches into the distance but, look left, and one sees the African or coloured location, a cluster of shabby dwellings, divided by dusty paths between barrack-style huts, under corrugated iron roofs, and overrun with children: crowded, ugly, insanitary. Look right, and there are lawns, bungalows, electric light, a church with its spire, a post office and police station — all the urban services of a charming small town. The unfree and the free — the former always outnumbering the latter. The African location is to the small town as Soweto is to Johannesburg: the country has taught the city its mechanism of control: 'Keep non-white labour close enough for employment but out of sight.'

Apartheid works. Or, rather, it worked in the past. It created homelands out of a jumbled pattern of geographical areas, corresponding roughly to the former Native Reserves. It endured the crisis years of Sharpeville and international criticism. It enforced control of the Republic against black protest. It was confident enough in the 1970s under Verwoerd's successor, Vorster, to reach out beyond its borders in an attempt at dialogue with a number of independent African states. It kept up the pretence that Europeans lived in the white Republic, Africans in the homelands. Citizenship could therefore be parcelled out by origin. The principal instruments of control were the pass laws, which, under a system of influx control, rid the white areas of 'illegals' — the black unemployed who were periodically forced back into their 'national states'. Their labour was needed, but their residence was conditional on their labour. Long-distance migration, and a shuttling back and forth from controlled locations to the industrial and mining centres, kept the system going. It was a remarkable fantasy, still heard today:

As far as political aspirations are concerned, the Government makes no distinction between urban Blacks and their compatriots in the self-governing national states. In terms of the policy of multinational development, all members of a given ethnonational group (such as the Zulus or Xhosas) exercise their political rights, including the vote, in their national states of origin, regardless of where they reside or work . . . In 1970 Parliament passed the National States Citizenship Act, which provides for a distinctive citizenship for each of the Black national states within the borders of South Africa. All Black men and women, irrespective of where in South Africa they live, are entitled to a certificate of their ethnonational state (*Yearbook 1984*, p. 216).

One should add a further characteristic of those Afrikaner apartheid years: its rage. Opposition was not simply rejected but fiercely resented. *'Ons voortrekkers het die land skoongemaak: ons is geregtig tot die vat van die land.'* ('Our forefathers cleared the land; we are entitled to the fat of the land.') What right had the world to point its finger at us? Why persecute us? The only explanation was the conspiracy of Marxist enemies who wished to pull down Christian South Africa. Communists! Strike first, reason afterwards. The government punished those, like the Revd Beyers Naudé, who spoke too boldly of reform, and crushed those who talked of the need for violence. One must note, too, the maturing of Afrikaner nationalism into something rather different. The National Party now began to be led by a state-centred elite which moderated its ethnic appeal and attracted support from English-speaking voters. The demise of Smuts's United Party was one indication of the change; the shift in voting patterns towards a *de facto* single-party system was another.

Such was the legacy of Verwoerd and Vorster, formulated in laws designed to control but presented as safeguards of European interests: the Mixed Marriage Act, section 16 of the Immorality Act, the pass laws, the Group Areas Act, the Registration of Population Act (through which people are designated, and sometimes redesignated, by race and colour), the Internal Security Act, the Political Interference Act (which limits membership of a political party to racial categories) and all their attendant legislation. The Verwoerd years also bequeathed the myth of the European majority in a plural society of minorities, an arithmetic of racial division which separated blacks into rival ethnic communities − a remarkable distortion which remains the basis of official policy.

It was into this world of fantasy that the present package of reforms had somehow to be inserted. Change was in the air, trying to find a way forward into the 1980s. How is it presented today?

It would be absurd to suppose that the past is being undone by politicians intent on revolution. The National Party is not like that. Mr Botha is not like that. Nor would white South Africa endorse change that was revolutionary. Such reforms as are allowed have more modest origins. One can list five likely sources. First, there is the actual momentum of change, the need to implement reforms recommended by numerous commissions which the government appointed towards the end of the 1970s, if only to be seen to be reformist: the Theron Commission, the Schlebush Commission, the Riekert Commission, the Wiehahn Commission. Second, there is the 'awful reality'[2] of the 22 million African population, who cannot be corralled into the national states if only because they are as desperate for work as the economy is desperate for their labour. Third, criticism by economists and the business sector, particularly the Chambers of Commerce, at a time of disquiet with the state of the economy, cannot be ignored. Fourth, the poverty of the national states, whether fully independent or self-governing, has to be faced. Fifth, there is the effect of external pressure, particularly from governments like those of Mr Reagan and Mrs Thatcher against which even an Afrikaner government finds it hard to bring the charge of 'liberalism'.

It is within these areas that we should look for clues to what President Botha is trying to do. They certainly do not point to revolution. They are predicated upon certain fundamental assumptions, notably, that white control of the Republic is permanent and inalienable. They are also linked to the past, though not to the immediate past. For one must recognize that apartheid is not the necessary centre of National Party politics. The innermost core is Afrikaner nationalism: everything is subordinate to that. And if the apartheid of Verwoerd or Vorster no longer serves the interests of Afrikaner nationalism, then apartheid too, at least in its 1960s formulation, is expendable. What remains is European control and Afrikaner leadership. In the twentieth century, political control requires some recognition of majority rule, and official theory is equal to that. If a majority is required, Europeans are designated the majority community in the plural world of white, African, coloured and Indian minorities. They are also of course a minority within the total population, but they are the majority-minority — a world of make-believe which the government still tries to insist is real.

1. The accumulation of reform

The commission under Professor Erika Theron of Stellenbosch was asked as early as 1973, when Vorster was prime minister, to inquire into the problems of the coloured community. Several attempts had been made to involve both coloureds and Indians at national level. The (coloured) Labour Party under Sonny Leon had declined to cooperate, and when in 1980 it refused to pass the budget for the Coloured Representative Council, the Council was dissolved. Meanwhile, the report of the Theron Commission was laid before parliament in 1976, and among its 220 resolutions was the recommendation that 'while the coloured people were an identifiable group, they should not be considered a distinct nation and the lines of their parallel development with the whites should be gradually narrowed.' The government havered, appointed a cabinet committee to consider the matter (one should not overlook the Afrikaner-Dutch capacity for bureaucratic delay), and then another commission of inquiry, from which a President's Council emerged to give precision to recommendations for a new constitution. The Theron Commission had reopened an old issue, touching the Afrikaner conscience in respect of the coloureds of the Western Cape — a Christian community whose mother tongue is Afrikaans. In 1956 the government had removed them from the common roll in the Cape and Natal; in 1968 it abolished their (white) representation in parliament. Here was an opportunity, therefore, to do something by way of restitution. The Indian community in Natal had fared no better. It was hemmed in and excluded, though that did not prevent the growth of a sizeable wealthy minority among them. A South African Indian Council of 21 nominated members had attracted little support. Why not, therefore, add the Indians to the coloureds to the whites in a new dispensation of reform? They would be two minorities alongside the white majority under a new constitution.

The outcome was the 1983 tricameral parliament, discussed later, and it would be wrong to dismiss the novelty of the change. Coloureds,

Indians and whites now have a common franchise, though in separate constituencies, throughout the Republic. They have representation at constituency level, cabinet level, in the electoral college for the President, in the President's Council, and on several statutory bodies. As we shall see, the constitution still conforms to theory. It is, in fact, a parliament of limited scope based on the formula 5:2:1 — five whites, two coloureds, one Indian — a constitution for majority-minority communities within the white Republic. It has upset conservative Afrikaners and it may yet raise awkward issues for the government. For if coloureds and Indians are raised to political equality with whites, what happens to the considerable body of legislation which enforces inequality under every other aspect of society — where men and women may live, whom they may marry, which schools their children must attend and which cemetery they will be buried in?

And what happens to blacks? If it is a measure of the government's change of policy that it is now eager to enlist some non-whites on the side of reform, how does it explain the inclusion of the 3 per cent of the population which is Indian and the exclusion of 70 per cent of the population which is African?

The official answer to this question is that Africans exercise their political rights in their national states, since South Africa is a 'multiethnic' federation of separate but equal peoples. Similarly, the labour migration of Africans into the Republic is said to be the equivalent of Mexicans entering the United States, or Algerians entering France, or Turks Germany. In practice, this kind of stance is no longer tenable. It is the policy of Canute's advisers to suppose not only that the flood of black labour can be kept back and controlled, but that it is morally sensible to do so. Economics has made nonsense of apartheid, and it is time (say economists) that it made sense of politics. So at least runs the tide of present criticism.

2. Black power

South Africa tries to regulate its citizens under an internal passport system comparable with that of the Soviet Union, and it would be wrong to conclude that the pass laws have not had an effect. The magistracy, police and administrative boards have forced many thousands of would-be migrants out of the Republic. But still their numbers grow and for obvious reasons: the rewards are high despite the penalties. A recent study of labour migration from Bophuthatswana produced the remarkable statistic, in itself an index of the realism beneath the pretence, that on plain actuarial calculations a semi-skilled worker could earn, illegally, five times more in three months in the Republic, plus nine months in prison, than if he were to work for a year in his own homeland. Everyone, therefore, may be said to be a citizen of somewhere, but the fact is that a majority of the African population will continue to live and toil in the Republic.[3] According to the 1984 *Yearbook* (p. 215), 'the percentage of South African Blacks living and working outside their traditional areas has increased with each population census. In 1960 only 38 per cent of all Blacks were in the White rural and urban areas. By 1970 the figure had grown to 53 per cent, and by 1980 to very nearly 60 per cent.' No matter how the statistics are adjusted, Africans in the Republic of South Africa outnumber whites, coloureds and Indians. It does not matter if blacks resident in the national states are excluded, the position is the same. It does not matter if migrants from Mozambique, Malawi and Angola, or from Lesotho, Botswana and Swaziland, are excluded, the picture is the same. Blacks outnumber whites and will do so increasingly. To quote the 1984 *Yearbook* again: 'A recent study by Dr Smit, Vice-President of the Human Sciences Research Council . . . shows that 50 per cent of South Africa's total urban population is Black and that if the current rate of Black urbanization is maintained, some 75 per cent will be urbanized by the year 2000. This means that 21 million additional Blacks will settle in urban areas in the next 20 years.'

It is the real world breaking in on the fantasy. A world of great hardship, for Africans do not enter the Republic as compact families of eager immigrants, but as contract labour, or as illegal workers on the outskirts of huddled townships, fearful of the police and of local bosses, having to evade the law which will endorse them or their families out of the Republic. They settle in huge caravanserai of squatters on the open veld, thousands upon tens of thousands, harried by the police, forced out from their encampments of cardboard and corrugated iron, enduring the freezing cold of winter and the heat of summer, without sanitation or comfort, women and men, children as well as parents; a permanent index of poverty in a society which has grown rich because of the labour of the poor. It is a world of Victorian squalor, of Tom-all-Alone's in an African setting.

Yet it is also a world of opportunity for those who find employment. Alongside the hardship there is the hope of betterment. Soweto is dreary, without charm, without grace, without trees, an enormous housing estate of dusty roads and crowded rooms, but offering the hope of livelihood despite the violence and exasperation of bureaucratic controls. (The violence is all too real: in recent years, excluding the actual months of rioting, there have been some four murders a day — one every six hours within the Soweto area.[4]) Within the townships there are enclaves of minimum luxury and maximum poverty. And, as the 1984 *Yearbook* points out (p. 480), they are permanent, part of the growing force of African labour on which industrial South Africa depends absolutely: 'Towards the year 2000 South Africa will have to rely more and more on the vast number of Black employees to make a bigger contribution, individually and collectively, to achieve the required growth in the economy and thus ensure that employment opportunities are available for the increasing number of entrants into the labour market.' The result is an accumulating power of purchase among Africans. Now, in the mid-1980s, they are outbuying Europeans. Such is the effect of the weight of numbers:

> . . . the Bureau of Market Research of the University of South Africa forecasts that by the end of the century the Black market will be twice the size of the total current market . . . By 1985 Blacks will account for 47.4 per cent of all private consumer spending compared with 36.3 per cent in 1979, while White consumer spending, currently 52.4 per cent of the total, will decline to 40.2 per cent. The Bureau also estimated that the Black population's share of total personal income rose from 22.5 per cent in 1970 to 25.9 per cent in 1975 and 29.1 per cent in 1980 (*Yearbook 1984*, p. 224).

3. Economic pressures

The world of South African business is fully aware of the change, and presses the government to come to terms with its needs. Listen, for example, to the Chairman of South African Breweries:

> There can be no doubt that the future of this consumer goods Company lies in Black spending. The politics and economics of this country are totally interwoven, so if one accepts that, one must concede that Black spending, as a percentage of the total, will continue to rise. On the retail side it is close to 50 per cent of the total and I believe in the next 10 years it will reach 75 per cent . . .

> Today South Africa is probably the only country worldwide which has the potential for a consumer explosion based on the fact that almost 80 per cent of our population will increase their real standards of living. SAB has invested much time, energy, money and marketing expertise in the Black market, where we are the dominant force today.

> We have set ourselves objectives in terms of training and development of Black executives, particularly at the middle management level, because that is where the hard core of our business lies . . . We are a R5 billion business — there is no way we are ever going to manage our business with White skills alone.[5]

Apartheid costs. It is inefficient as well as cruel: 'At the root of our problem is the rootlessness of our workers. And it costs — in excessive non-productive training time, in unskilled workmanship. In failure to meet deadlines. In the constraints it places on quoting for contracts . . .'[6]

In September 1984 the Johannesburg *Financial Mail* launched a major attack on influx control. It was directed against 'the ideology of the former Prime Minister Verwoerd . . . The cost of this mad dream has been high in terms of economic opportunities squandered, human misery inflicted and international anger.' Hundreds of thousands of blacks had been moved or threatened with resettlement by the 'clearance of black spots'.[7] The Urban Foundation was quoted in defence of the argument that influx control was not actually needed: those already employed were not asking for its protection, and most of the migrants who, it was feared, would flood to the cities either were already there or would continue to move back and forth to the homelands. 'The number of migrants who would urbanize permanently is fairly limited', or would be if the government did not harass them.[8] Almost surely, that omits the number of dependants and new migrants who would be attracted to the cities if there were a free market, but it is the economic case for ending influx control which has been urged by men like Gavin Relly, Chairman of Anglo-American. The *Financial Mail* again:

> In South Africa, influx control is a major impediment not only to economic growth but to the new consensus politics. If government is serious about addressing itself to reform, the system must go. Indeed its demise is imperative for economic and political reasons alike.
>
> In effect influx control is an attempt — which is failing — to bar urbanization to millions of Black South Africans. Urbanization, which the country desperately needs for economic reasons, takes place anyway. But in attempting to arrest the process, millions of people are criminalized, untold suffering and bitterness are created, and respect for the law is lost.[9]

Rational argument rarely offers much to politicians, but that the South African economy is changing no one disputes. As more Africans are drawn into industry and commerce, they are doing skilled jobs at relatively low cost. Whether they will displace some whites or simply push them higher up the economic ladder is an argument we must examine later.[10] The National Party, too, has had to adapt. It is no longer the voice of the poor Afrikaner, if indeed it was ever that, but of party-bureaucrats, professional men, corporation managers, business interests and the urban middle class. There are some in the party, therefore, who listen to economic arguments, but most party members, like the white community in general, still hold closely to an economically privileged existence.

4. The national states

It was the dream of men like Verwoerd that national states of black workers could be strategically placed to serve white South Africa. New industries would be sited on their borders, and new African leaders with whom Pretoria could negotiate would emerge to displace the African National Congress (ANC). It was plausible only if one shut one's eyes to the map, which showed divided homelands scattered throughout the huge area of the Republic. Successive governments went ahead with the policy — native reserves becoming Bantustans becoming national states. In a speech to the party convention in Cape Town, late in 1984, President Botha beat his breast. 'If only', he said, 'we had taken the Tomlinson Commission more seriously.' It was an odd admission, showing how ambivalent the present government is about the past. Had the 1955 Tomlinson Commission been implemented fully, the national states would be better placed economically today, but no government was prepared to pay the cost.[11] Meanwhile, the present administration has tried to consolidate the fragmented areas. It hopes to 'reduce the total number of component units from 98 to 28 by means of exchange and purchase',[12] but it is not easy. In 1980, for example, the town of Mafeking, on the border of one part of Bophuthatswana (more renowned in British than in Afrikaner history), was transferred to African rule, but when a similar proposal was made to incorporate King Williams Town into the Ciskei, the ratepayers objected and that was that: it remains an island of wealth encircled by the poverty of Ciskei. Consolidation has also produced the enforced relocation of Africans from 'black spots' within the Republic. Some 3 million Africans — an astonishing number — have been settled from white to black areas, and most estimates indicate that the government intends to transfer a further 2 million.[13]

It is an old truth that 70 per cent of the population of South Africa is black and has less than 13 per cent of the land that it can legally call its own. The division was fixed in 1913 and confirmed in 1936. Now there is a new dispensation, but of all the issues that disturb the Afrikaner soul, land is pre-eminently the most sensitive: little is done because no government dares give reality to what is fantasy. By the beginning of the 1980s, 'land purchase and exchange' had not even filled the 1936 quota. One can see why. The national states could be viable only if they were enlarged economically and geographically at white South Africa's expense. We have Mr Botha's declaration (*Yearbook 1984*, p. 207): 'In most of the national states less than 20 per cent of the population derive their income from their geographic area and we simply cannot hand over the entire republic of South Africa merely to establish viable Black states.'

They are also unattractive politically. There is a murderous competition for power in Venda and Ciskei, corruption in Transkei. The most interesting is KwaZulu, where a local leader has indeed arisen — Chief Gatsha Buthelezi — and it is ironic that the government does not find it easy to do business with him. Through his Zulu-based Inkatha movement, Buthelezi has laid claim to more than his KwaZulu homelands. He opposes the 1983 constitution, joins forces with the Progressive Federal Party (PFP) in demanding power-sharing between black and white throughout South Africa, and has given his name to the Buthelezi Commission: in 1982 it set out proposals for political cooperation between KwaZulu and Natal which brought sharp condemnation from the government. Given to pithy sayings — 'apartheid lives on the borrowed time of black disunity' — Buthelezi is more an embarrassment to the government than an alternative to the ANC, but he is also a portent for the future in the sense that the national states are not going to fade away or be disbanded. They are still fundamental to government policy, and they are sufficiently established now to have built a network of interests among those who profit from them:

> . . . it is indisputable that a stratum of blacks is emerging which is materially better off than perhaps any that has existed in those territories since Union and directly dependent on white capital . . . Research has been reported on the extent to which the participants in the political institutions of the Bantustans, members of the legislative assemblies, ministers, senior civil servants and chiefs have had substantial and continuous pay increases — all tending to confirm that a layer of the black population was both being enriched and bought off from any tendency to radical opposition they might entertain.[14]

That is surely true. One can see the phenomenon in independent Africa, of small states overloaded with government elites who rule impoverished farmers. There was a time when the homelands could at least feed their population. Now the continuing drought and the dispatch of unwanted, unemployed Africans from the Republic have reduced whole areas of the national states to a rural slum. To journey through the Ciskei or across the separated territories of Bophuthatswana is to see not how little is being tried but how little can be done without massive expenditure.[15] The governments of the national states protest from time to time over policies enforced by Pretoria, including the consequences of influx control — Kaiser Matanzima in the Transkei actually 'broke off diplomatic relations' between Umtata and Pretoria in 1981 — but they are dwarfs struggling against a giant.[16]

5. *International pressures*

In that same address to the Cape Town conference the President made a further admission: 'Criticism from outside South Africa,' he told delegates, 'from those who are not its enemies, cannot be disregarded.' In a sense it was a truism, since the condition of South Africa has always made it sensitive to changes in world markets and capital movements. But there is now a larger concern about the consequences of rupture between white South Africa and those whom the government would like to see as allies. It does not prevent disagreements between Pretoria and London or Washington, but the dependence of the Republic on external trade is even more striking than its reliance on foreign capital: by 1982 imports amounted to 31 per cent of the national income.[17]

Since the mid-1970s a new worry has grown. The United States has entered the arena. The failure of Portuguese rule and the arrival of the Cubans brought in the superpowers, and relations between Pretoria and Washington are awkward for both sides, not least because of the vulnerability of the United States to domestic pressure from black Americans. It is true that neither South Africa, nor Africa as a whole, is given any great priority in the range of American or Soviet interests, but the apprehension of Afrikaner leaders is that once again they are facing the unpredictable strength of a great power.

Socially, too, South Africa is a penetrated state. It cannot seal itself off from the world. Newspapers from abroad, broadcasts from overseas, the television screen, video films, the popular music that brings ambiguous messages of love and freedom as part of the youth culture of the twentieth century, cannot be blanketed out despite government control of the media. The Republic wants very much to be part of the West. It is why sanctions on sporting fixtures truly hurt the ordinary white South African, not least the Afrikaner, and why measures taken by Washington, London or Brussels, affecting investment and the employment of African workers cannot wholly be ignored.

The weight of each of these different elements – the complications of the international world, the national states, the economy, the influx of African labour, and the causal sequence of events – presses on the government, forcing recognition of the need to change at least the formulation of policy. Each compounds the others and adds to the urgency to do something. The National Party claims to have achieved, or to be about to achieve, a large measure of reform, and it is possible to draw up a list of innovations: (i) a new constitution; (ii) recognition of African trade unions; (iii) the easing of restrictions on black labour, including abolition of the coloured preference quota in the Western Cape; (iv) recognition of some blacks as – to use South African terminology – permanent residents in the Republic; (v) the lifting of restrictions on some aspects of African business; (vi) the appointment of a cabinet committee to consider the question of 'black political rights' in the Republic; and (vii) the prospect of ending 'hurtful aspects' of apartheid, such as the Mixed Marriage Act and section 16 of the Immorality Act forbidding sexual relations between white and non-white.

The list is almost as much promise as achievement. Liberal elements within the Afrikaner community, particularly the PFP, deride such reforms and argue the need for a national forum of all communities to determine future policies. Others are shocked by what they hear and have quit the National Party to try to set a boundary to further change. We should look briefly at the revolt of the conservative Afrikaner before assessing what is being done.

An obvious point that is sometimes overlooked by kindly observers is that South Africans are not liberal democrats. They have had a different upbringing, particularly if they are Afrikaans-speaking. They are not Whigs. Their soul was forged in a harsher world, and they hold its beliefs dear. That is why Mr Botha is disturbing. Where is he going, they ask, and what is he doing?

In conservative eyes, the government is demythologizing the party. A useful exercise, one might think, but also dangerous. A society as uneasy in its history as white South Africa needs all the myths it can preserve if it is to survive. The laager, the trek and an insistence on white supremacy are vital to the Afrikaner view of the world. It is a view that some believe Mr Botha is trying to reduce. To become merely the dominant party in a tricameral legislature, they say, is to engage in the politics of wheeler-dealing: a government which promises political rights to Africans within the Republic does not know what it is doing or, if it does, it must be prepared to see the Afrikaner community divided as it has not been since 1948. It is a betrayal, a dangerous betrayal, since promises of that kind arouse expectations that cannot be met. Pragmatism has never been enough in the long history of South Africa's Afrikaners, and Botha (say his critics) should read de Tocqueville on the dangers of concessions which are never able to satisfy the appetite they arouse.[18]

What worries men like Dr Andries Treurnicht, former chairman of the NP in the Transvaal and now leader of the new Conservative Party, are the very presuppositions which Mr Botha believes will ensure survival: that, for example, the Republic can be redefined to include coloureds and Indians, and that the grievances of Africans must be met by constitutional as well as economic reforms. If such beliefs are held, it is asked, why should the government stop at trade union rights or residence rights? The next step must surely be voting rights. Why stop at power-sharing among whites, coloureds and Indians? Where is the breakwater to halt the onward rush of liberal reform to majority rule and a black government? It can exist, says Treurnicht, only if a line is drawn and held in defence of white South Africa. Otherwise, one is loosening the stones at the top of the slope, there will be nothing to check the avalanche that follows, and one might as well pull down the Voortrekker Monument and the national flag of the Republic before they are both overwhelmed by black power.

No more than a minority of white voters accepts logic of that order, but it is a minority which has grown since Mr Botha announced his programme of reform. The National Party still occupies a huge central area of the political arena, but the government is not fully at ease. The right-wing opposition is more firmly based among the electorate than it is in parliament, the NP is more dependent than before on English-speaking voters. When in February 1982 the parliamentary caucus of the party was asked to vote on a motion of confidence in P.W. Botha as leader, and to give approval to proposals for constitutional reform, 22 members refused. (Six later recanted, sixteen remained opposed.)

They included Dr Treurnicht, then minister for state administration, and Dr Hartzenberg, minister for education. Dr Connie Mulder added his support. Such was the origin of the Conservative Party and its 28 members in the present House of Assembly.[19]

What are the reforms that the government uses as evidence of change? They cover three broad areas: the constitution, the labour market, and aspects of social policy which (it is claimed) will lead the country away from apartheid.

A. The constitution

The new parliament is strange, a form of constitutional apartheid tempered by necessity. When Englishmen talk politics they talk class, but when South Africans talk politics they talk race. The litany runs through every attempt at reform. Thus the arithmetic of race is used to construct the new republic. Africans are excluded not because they have tribal homelands, though that is a convenient half-truth, but because they are numerous. It is feared that, given any form of political leverage, they will turn the racial pyramid upside down, leaving those on top — the whites — crushed at the bottom. In theory, blacks do not form a single community, being divided by tribal nationalisms; in practice, the government fears that all Africans are black and, therefore, hostile to whites. So they are excluded. The problem of 'black political rights' for Africans who live in the 'white Republic' may be high on the list of government preoccupations, but whatever form such a concession might take, it is unlikely to be a fourth House of the People, proportionate to population, within a quadripartite legislature. According to the 1984 *Yearbook* (p. 199),

> There were really only two courses open to the country. First there was integration, which implied that the institutions of government should gradually if not immediately be opened to Blacks as well, and that political power should be shared on the basis of adult suffrage with full representation for all in a common society. The alternative was the purposive development of political practices fashioned by three centuries of experience in Africa so that parallel institutions of government and administration could materialize for

the Black peoples through which they could reach autonomy and assume full responsibility for their own affairs.

This is a clear expression of the Afrikaner commitment to separation, to a state based on race rather than class. The leaders are anti-Marxists who believe in the reality of class war but see it always in terms of race: the black proletariat subjugating the white middle class. 'For one thing', the *Yearbook* continues, 'such a form of integration would mean a new kind of colonial subjugation of the White nation, for in a so-called common society it would no longer be master of its own political and economic destiny. And if it is wrong for a Black people to be subjected to a colonial power it must be equally wrong for a White nation to be so subjugated.'

The constitution stops well short of integration, and merely alters the dividing line between the races by extending the vote on a national basis to all non-Africans. It has always been possible to add up the racial numbers in different ways, since in the uneven balance between black and white the smaller weights of 2.7 million coloureds and 870,000 Indians can be moved to one end or the other. The equation can be either:

Non-Whites: 25.6 million	*versus*	Whites: 4.5 million
(Africans, Coloureds, Indians)		

or

Africans: 22 million	*versus*	Non-Africans: 8 million
		(Whites, Coloureds, Indians)

The constitution tilts the balance towards the 8 million, seeking to appeal to the minority communities, not only on the basis of their relative advantage — Indians more than coloureds, coloureds more than Africans — but through the offer of a national, though divided, legislature:

House of Assembly — European	178 members*
House of Representatives — Coloured	85 members
House of Delegates — Indian	45 members

* Within each House there are a number of additional members: eight elected plus four nominated in the Assembly; three elected plus two nominated in the other Houses.

The parliament has three separate chambers, each with its own executive council of four or five ministers, in addition to the president's executive cabinet of 20 ministers. There is an electoral college of 50 elected whites, 25 coloureds and 13 Indians. It met on 5 September 1984 and elected P.W. Botha as the new republic's first president. The office of prime minister disappears, and an executive-style president chooses his cabinet from all three chambers. He also takes advice from the President's Council of 60 members — 20 designated by the House of Assembly, 10 by the House of Representatives, 5 by the House of Delegates (including members from majority and minority parties) and 25 appointed by the president.

The draft constitution was approved by a two-thirds majority in the former white parliament in September 1983 and endorsed by white voters in a referendum on 2 November: 'Yes' votes, 66 per cent; 'No' votes, 33.5 per cent; spoilt papers, 0.5 per cent. The government argued that it had moved closer to democracy (*South African Newsletter*, October 1983, no. 10):

> The year 1983 marks a departure from the present whites-only Westminster-orientated parliament, which is basically a conflict-style government with a winner-takes-all-approach that amounts to a dictatorship of the majority in a multi-ethnic society, in favour of a more democratic dispensation in which everyone, both individually and within his own community, will have an effective say in decisions affecting his own interests.

The theory behind such claims is the rather tired notion of consociational democracy, the evocation of a coalition through which the leaders of a communally divided society cooperate without merging their particular interests: it is a process of bargaining through elite accommodation. It is also reinforced by concepts of a plural society in which the Republic of South Africa and its tricameral parliament stand in juxtaposition to a loose association of African national states (*e pluribus plures*?), on whose labour the whole of southern Africa depends (*e pluribus unum*?). It is, however, a strangely qualified form of consociation, for it has no common assembly in which agreements among representatives of the plural society can be worked out. It is incorporation at arm's length, a political oddity even in a land used to fantasy, under a constitution which excludes the black majority in order to preserve a white/coloured/Indian ratio of 5:2:1.

A distinctive feature of this arrangement is the attempt to distinguish between 'own affairs' and 'general affairs'. The former are those which constitute, in theory, the separated group interests of whites, coloureds or Indians – education, health, social welfare, local government and certain aspects of agriculture – set out in a schedule to the constitution. Legislation in each of the three chambers has to be certified by the president as dealing exclusively with the 'own affairs' of the population in question, but none of the Houses has the power to levy taxes or raise loans in order to finance its own affairs. That belongs to 'general affairs', the province of the president and his cabinet. On the other hand, Bills on matters of common concern have to be approved by each House voting separately. If they cannot agree – if one or two Houses reject a Bill, or the Houses pass different amended versions of the Bill – the president can refer the disputed measure to his council, whose arbitration will be final: its decision is deemed to be a Bill passed by parliament.

This process is so tortuous that the gulf between the three communities may be bridged by the sheer necessity to cooperate. Indeed the key to the clumsy procedures outlined in the constitution is said to lie in 'consensus' by negotiation through joint standing committees and joint sessions (same issue of the *Newsletter*):

> Legislation on matters of common concern must be approved by all three chambers sitting separately [but] unanimity among the three chambers will be enhanced if matters of common concern, including legislation, are referred to joint standing committees. The approach will not be conflict-centred and winner-takes-all, but it will ring in an era of consensus-style government in South Africa. In the new dispensation, negotiation will be of vital importance.

Such a *ménage à trois* would certainly be a triumph of hope over experience. In fact, the constitution does not leave much to chance. It is hedged about with qualifications over and above the veto power (by weight of numbers) of the white House of Assembly. If, for example, any of the three Houses cannot or will not cooperate when called upon by proclamation of the president to do so – if, that is, there is a boycott of proceedings – then parliament shall consist of the House or Houses that are able to perform their functions. *Les absents ont toujours tort.*

And if parliament cannot act, the president will. For the other major feature of the constitution is the shift to an executive presidency. The change was already implicit in the drift towards single-party rule, reflecting both the monopoly of power by the National Party and the authority of the leader under a succession of dominant prime ministers.[20] It seems reasonable to assume that the locus of power has moved to a Gaullist-style presidency so as to make sure that the multi-legislative system is subject to a regulatory power. The effect has been to modify the former Westminster style of government. Ministers for 'general affairs' are still responsible to one or other of the chambers; those in charge of departments of state are drawn at present from the European House of Assembly. (The chairmen of the ministerial councils in the House of Representatives and the House of Delegates – the Revd Allan Hendrickse and Mr Amichand Rajbansi – are ministers without portfolio in the cabinet; the chairman of the council of ministers in the House of Assembly is also the minister of health and welfare at national level.) But the president sits above all three legislatures. He is chairman not only of the cabinet but of the National Intelligence Service (which includes the State Security Council), the President's Council and the Committee of Priorities for new legislation. He also controls his own small secretariat. It is Downing Street-plus-the-White House under local labels.

It was imprudent, however, of the government to have been so confident in its wooing of its new electorates. It believed that it had the cooperation of the (coloured) Labour Party and the (Indian) National People's Party, although it was not long ago that both communities were disparaged. The latter were held to be unassimilable, the former were said to be degenerate. Both communities are still incensed by the apartheid of inferior education, poor job opportunities, low wages, restrictions on everyday life, and the enforced removal of families from their traditional homes.[21] The riots which spread from Soweto in 1976 were not confined to Africans. They involved sections of the coloureds, led by students and school children, among whom the police acted as brutally as they had in the African townships. Indians, too, though fearful of black resentment, remembering the riots which set fire to Durban in 1949, have joined forces from time to time with both Africans and coloureds, out of a tradition of protest which goes back to Gandhi.[22]

When elections took place for the House of Representatives and the House of Delegates (membership of the House of Assembly was extended to 1989), the results were disappointing for the government. At the end of the two days' voting (23 and 28 August 1984), each side to the contest claimed some sort of success, although the result may turn out to be like Caspar's memory of Blenheim: ''Twas a famous victory', but no one quite knew why.

	Eligible (a)	*Registered (b)*	*Voters*
Coloureds	1,500,058	911,931	209,791 (14% of 'a'; 23% of 'b')
Indians	504,400	411,804	83,703 (16.6% of 'a'; 20.3% of 'b')

The Labour Party under Allan Hendrickse won an easy majority of seats in the House of Representatives. Amichand Rajbansi was less fortunate in the House of Delegates, where a quarrel broke out among members, the leaders wooing various factions in the hope of securing a majority for themselves. The struggle was determined by the fact that the chairmen of the three ministerial councils (as leaders of the majority in each House) were to be members of the president's cabinet. Opposition to the election came from two broad multiracial coalitions. One was the United Democratic Front (UDF), sympathetic to the ideals of the banned ANC; the other was the National Forum, which looked back to the Black Consciousness movement (also banned) of Steve Biko and the Pan-Africanist Congress (PAC). The government reacted angrily towards those who tried to persuade the electorate not to vote. It detained leaders of the UDF and banned all political meetings whether public or private. It seems likely, however, that the rewards of office, including membership of a national legislature, ministerial positions and a seat on the President's Council, will carry the constitution forward for a time on its strange, three-legged base.

Consensus government remained illusory. The rhino whip, birdshot, tear gas, sneeze machines, plastic bullets, real bullets, detention orders, arrests, stone-throwing, petrol bombs and concerted abuse — all the familiar accompaniments of non-white protest and police reaction — welcomed the dawn of consociational democracy. The inauguration of Mr Botha as president in September 1984 was orderly within the Assembly at Cape Town. His address to the three combined Houses of Parliament, when it was not always easy to distinguish the Aryan Indians from the more swarthy Afrikaners, was full of invocations to God and assurances of concern for all South Africans, including the non-represented black population. Meanwhile, in the northern Cape, the army was conducting Operation Thunder Chariot, the largest military manoeuvres since 1945. The police arrested members of the Natal Indian Congress and the UDF, six of whose members fled into the British consulate in Durban.[23] Louis le Grange, minister for law and order, imposed a blanket ban on meetings in the Pretoria/Witwatersrand area, and black smoke from burning schools and offices hung over the mining townships, where a strike among gold miners, legal under the new dispensation, had turned into an armed clash between workers and police.

The constitution ought to be by way of a promissory note. If it is to work fully, and the chances cannot be very good, it needs to reward its new voters; and if it is to survive in the long term, a still more doubtful case, some provision will have to be made for the excluded African majority. They must be either offered alternative benefits, or kept forcibly under control, or divided and ruled by some combination of stick and carrot. The government can see the immensity of the problem, but can it deliver? Its defenders argue that it has in fact begun to do so, particularly in respect of labour and employment.

B. The labour market

National Party leaders are sufficiently anglicized today to want to employ commissions of inquiry. Two are well known, those of Riekert and Wiehahn.[24] Their reports are interesting, since they concern the central domestic problem of South Africa in the 1980s: namely, whether the needs of a unified economy can be met within the framework of limited political rights. The party raises the banner of reform, but the compulsion is largely economic. It comes from the demand for a stable, properly trained workforce, and that can be supplied only from among Africans who struggle to become wage and salary earners within the Republic. The obstacles they encounter are politically imposed − influx control, segregated townships, inferior education, a limited apprenticeship, poor housing, rising rents and the expense of travel to and from employment − but in the tug of argument between politics and economics, politicians have by no means lost the battle.

In general, both Riekert and Wiehahn tried to mitigate the effects of apartheid legislation. They looked for a middle road of reform between 'total segregation and total incorporation' under a 'free enterprise system' (Mr Botha's phrases), and for ways of strengthening the urban African middle class − middle in the sense of wealth, class in the sense of life-style. Wanting to rationalize the labour market, they proposed to free Africans who entered the market economy from as many restrictive measures as the government would allow. The hope was double: to ease the lot of migrant labour, and to confer economic rewards so as to blunt political demands. Official statements have been naively optimistic (*Yearbook 1984*, p. 222): 'Obviously the best way to neutralize the appeal of Marxist promises would be to allow private initiative free play . . . The 'economic cake' must be seen to be available to all with the ability to claim their share on merit. Hence the many initiatives by Mr Botha's government to open up new opportunities for urban Blacks.'

The chief interest of the Wiehahn Commission on Labour Legislation lay in its recommendation that African trade unions, illegally in existence for many years, should be officially registered and, therefore, able to take strike action. When presented with the report, the government hesitated, then conceded the right by a series of amending acts between 1979 and 1982. The Report also stressed the need to get rid of a number of restrictions − to desegregate facilities in shops and factories, to increase training for African labour and to provide industrial courts to settle disputes irrespective of race. Similarly, the Riekert Commission on the Utilization of Manpower tried 'to improve the use of black labour in the country's free market system'. It, too, recommended reforms, including the right of Africans to a 99-year lease on property, improvements in electricity supply within the townships, the encouragement of

29

private capital to build houses for non-whites, a more rational system of labour bureaux, the right of all races to skilled employment (that is, no job reservation) and the ending of apartheid in hotels, restaurants, concert halls and sports grounds wherever local managers wished to do so.

In many ways, the two reports tried to give a push forward to existing trends, but when the Riekert Commission looked at fundamental reform, it drew back. The main impediment to the free movement of labour has been the government's own policy of influx control. The business sector (as we have seen) wants an end to it, but the Commission disagreed, arguing that enforcement of the pass laws was necessary. There was a need, it said, to regulate the numbers of those who would otherwise crowd out those in work, while any increase in unemployment would add to violence in the townships. The caution was predictable. Reform under restraint, and economics yielding to politics, are at the heart of the South African dilemma – a situation made worse by a government which behaves in the last quarter of the twentieth century as Western governments once behaved in the distant past.[25]

As some Africans become better off, is there any basis for the hope that economic reforms will moderate political demands? The answer seems to be that it might happen if there were evidence of a substantial increase in African living standards. But the statistics of race and occupation, wage rates and social mobility do not support the picture of overall improvement that government spokesmen like to present.

The plain fact is that whereas whites, Asians and coloureds have improved their share of the labour market, Africans have not. True, there are more Africans in employment, but there are also more unemployed, if only because of the numbers seeking work (see Table 1). During the decade 1970–80 (that is, even before the worst of the current recession), unemployment grew by 300,000 – though not among whites or Asians – alongside a workforce that increased by one and a quarter million. During that decade, whites gained almost 10,000 jobs, Asians some 2,000; coloureds lost 1,000 jobs, but still improved their overall position. By contrast, blacks lost over 400,000 jobs, and saw their position grow worse. The minority communities gained, therefore, at the expense of Africans. Nor is the ratio of wages between the four communities quite so hopeful as it is often argued to be (see Table 2). The gap has narrowed, but it remains very large, offset (according to official comment) to the advantage of blacks because of their relatively young age, but still more offset, surely, to their detriment by all the advantages of being white, in the form of pensions, mortgage relief, subsidized benefits and social security payments.

If one turns from the official statistics to private surveys, the picture is bleak. The Carnegie study of poverty, directed by Professor Francis Wilson, reached two tentative conclusions from the mass of data still being analysed.[26] There were now 'nearly nine million blacks living below the minimum subsistence level in the homelands, the number having doubled in the past 20 years; those without any income stood at 1.43 million in 1980 compared with a quarter of a million in 1960.' The situation was obviously better in the Republic itself, though poverty, disease and hunger were widespread in the rural areas. In the cities 'those blacks who by accident of birth and the good fortune of continuous employment have established tenuous legal rights have been able to improve their standards of living in the past 20 years, but many still live close to the poverty line in overcrowded, insecure townships, *and as a relatively privileged group they are a diminishing proportion of blacks in South Africa.*' The explanation of both statements is simple. It is the result of influx control, restricted land use and the absence of citizenship rights.

Where, then, is the basis for any optimism about the decade to come? It springs from three beliefs. One is that because the number of Africans in employment has risen, and is bound to rise further, many more are better off and therefore have reason not to rebel. Second, there is the belief that Africans are acquiring new skills, including those of a managerial and professional kind, at a correspondingly high level of remuneration: a new managerial class has sprung up, growing from 180,000 to some 370,000 over the past ten years. Third, there is the compound belief that a middle level of African wealth is slowly being established as a buffer between the poverty of the mass and the privileges of the white minority, a belief that African middle-class-morality-plus-television-sets-and-washing-machines will be a stabilizing influence on the politics, as well as on the economics, of South African society.

The hope is supported by many leaders of South African industry and commerce. But it is prudent to set alongside it three contrary factors. First, as shown in the Carnegie study, there are the very large

Table 1 Distribution of workforce over major employment sectors, 1970–80

Sector	Year	Total		Whites		Coloureds		Asians		Blacks	
Agriculture, forestry, fishing	1970	2,012,296	100	97,822	4.9	116,725	5.8	7,317	0.4	1,790,432	88.9
	1980	1,299,840	100	102,560,	7.9	149,240	11.5	7,740	0.6	1,040,300	80.0
Mining and quarrying	1970	641,597	100	62,414	9.7	7,517	1.1	720	0.1	571,306	89.1
	1980	820,300	100	90,120	11.0	12,660	1.6	1,820	0.2	715,700	87.2
Manufacturing	1970	1,005,749	100	281,469	28.0	166,007	16.5	64,448	6.4	493,825	49.1
	1980	1,456,760	100	360,980	24.8	227,500	15.6	96,560	6.6	771,720	53.0
Electricity, gas and water	1970	45,123	100	14,155	31.4	2,475	5.5	204	0.5	28,289	62.6
	1980	79,240	100	29,360	36.7	6,600	8.9	920	1.3	42,360	53.1
Construction	1970	447,679	100	97,763	21.8	78,469	17.5	9,142	2.1	262,305	58.6
	1980	452,440	100	101,540	22.6	78,920	17.5	11,440	2.4	260,540	57.5
Commerce	1970	680,681	100	268,576	39.5	76,507	11.2	50,813	7.5	284,785	41.8
	1980	1,008,340	100	299,060	29.7	104,620	10.3	65,700	6.4	538,960	53.6

Transport and communication	1970	329,397	100	164,455	50.0	27,472	8.3	7,286	2.2	130,184	39.5
	1980	424,040	100	192,360	45.2	38,180	9.0	13,600	3.3	179,900	42.5
Finance	1970	187,852	100	143,288	76.3	6,834	3.6	2,864	1.5	34,866	18.6
	1980	285,840	100	208,400	72.8	15,200	5.2	9,700	3.5	52,540	18.5
Services	1970	1,517,609	100	323,220	21.3	159,255	10.5	22,341	1.5	1,012,793	66.7
	1980	1,986,240	100	479,900	24.1	211,380	10.7	33,720	1.7	1,261,240	63.5
Unemployed and other	1970	538,851	100	50,574	9.4	72,922	13.5	16,492	3.1	298,863	74.0
	1980	852,660	100	40,780	4.8	83,480	9.7	14,620	1.8	713,780	83.7
TOTAL	1970	7,406,834	100	1,503,736	20.3	713,823	9.6	181,627	2.5	5,007,648	67.6
	1980	8,665,700	100	1,905,060	22.0	927,780	10.7	255,820	3.0	5,577,040	64.3

Note: The figures for 1980, taken from the 1980 population census, are based on a 5 per cent sample and exclude Transkei, Bophuthatswana and Venda; those for 1970 are based on the whole population and include these areas.
Source: Republic of South Africa, Central Statistical Services, *Bulletin of Statistics*, 1982.

Table 2 Average monthly earnings in various sectors, 1972–82

Industrial sector and population group	1972 R	1973 R	1974 R	1975 R	1976 R	1977 R	1978 R	1979 R	1980 R	1981 R	1982 R
Whites: Total	317	349	398	449	491	535	585	655	767	936	1,090
Mining	402	475	563	636	713	771	839	923	1,035	1,231	1,416
Manufacturing	362	389	449	510	571	624	700	805	956	1,133	1,313
Electricity	395	426	494	567	592	651	694	800	982	1,163	1,375
Construction	380	410	445	506	557	639	734	815	949	1,133	1,329
Trade and accommodation services	244	262	290	320	350	400	439	488	549	711	842
Transport and communications	307	359	407	469	506	522	555	627	748	949	1,067
Finance and insurance	306	341	400	467	516	566	630	681	789	920	1,012
Government and services	310	345	394	434	454	455	525	573	677	820	983
Coloureds: Total	97	111	125	144	159	174	191	210	254	310	367
Mining	76	103	137	159	186	210	231	274	318	366	451
Manufacturing	92	104	118	134	154	173	191	220	263	317	372
Electricity	103	114	132	214	175	222	239	284	347	471	408
Construction	127	141	160	192	217	221	236	227	282	344	407
Trade and accommodation services	79	89	98	110	122	138	152	176	205	251	287
Transport and communications	81	99	118	132	125	135	148	161	214	247	302
Finance and insurance	113	129	154	185	212	242	270	302	344	457	520
Government and services	113	133	141	161	168	177	198	210	257	315	388

Asians: Total	112	127	145	170	195	221	250	278	336	411	537
Mining	115	133	170	206	275	288	348	411	439	592	658
Manufacturing	98	111	128	153	183	203	229	250	299	359	516
Electricity	–	–	–	–	–	–	–	–	–	–	503
Construction	167	188	213	254	270	318	352	402	465	532	663
Trade and accommodation services	108	121	136	153	168	205	230	251	302	369	449
Transport and communications	127	138	164	193	209	220	242	277	354	519	770
Finance and insurance	180	203	210	247	289	321	357	390	466	579	679
Government and services	144	169	199	232	259	282	335	363	451	596	727
Blacks: Total	48	57	72	91	107	121	137	156	189	228	296
Mining	22	29	45	74	88	100	118	138	172	212	252
Manufacturing	62	71	88	106	125	141	161	187	224	271	415
Electricity	86	80	100	119	132	155	166	183	223	274	368
Construction	61	71	84	104	112	124	131	147	178	206	244
Trade and accommodation services	53	59	66	77	90	105	115	127	149	177	210
Transport and communications	51	68	82	93	108	118	133	160	203	243	277
Finance and insurance	77	94	118	145	163	194	211	237	282	337	393
Government services	51	61	74	88	103	116	136	153	182	220	248

Source: As for Table 1.

numbers of Africans who live on or below a minimal proverty datumline even in the townships which serve industrial/commercial areas. The Pretoria/Witwatersrand/Vereeniging area (writes Mr Pillay, one of the Carnegie survey's research workers) is 'a universe of poverty'. An area of over 5 million inhabitants − 1.8 million whites, 3 million-plus blacks − it has an unemployment rate among Africans of almost 30 per cent, including 25 per cent who have never been employed. There is overcrowding, disease, violence, mental illness and extremes of poverty. Yet the black population in the area is expected to increase to 9 million early in the next century. Similarly, in the south of the country, about a third of black children were found by Dr John Hansen, of the University of Witwatersrand, to be underweight and stunted: 'In some areas, such as parts of the Ciskei and Chatworth in Durban, the situation is worse, rising to 60 or 70 per cent or more.' In brief, if there is a growing degree of affluence among black workers, there is also a large degree of misery among millions of black households.

Second, the number of Africans who have taken up apprenticeship schemes is still very small. According to the 1984 *Yearbook* (Table 22, p.492), between 1972 and 1982 the number of blacks, 'newly indentured as apprentices', rose from 82 to 741, whereas whites increased their number from 7,363 to 10,659 − from, of course, a much smaller workforce. The Manpower Training Act (the first non-discriminating act, established as a result of the Wiehahn Report) was passed only in 1981. If the number of Africans undergoing short courses in training centres is added, the picture (in 1982) is better: blacks 98,600, whites 94,240 − but how inadequate is the provision against the need.*

* In September 1983, the *Financial Mail* carried a 'Manpower Survey on Training'. Current needs were for some 20,000 new artisans a year, but 'the overall percentage in the workforce will decline because companies have cut back on their bursaries during the recession. The effect will show up in four years' time . . . The future supply of black engineers will be a trickle.' Meanwhile the 'inadequate black educational system has provided a massive stream of people who are simply incapable of being satisfactorily trained . . . It could be the end of the century before there is any recognizable improvement . . . Blacks still find it difficult to penetrate into management. When they do enter they either find it hard to cope or to be taken seriously.' Most of the non-whites (trained as managers by Shell) who earn R14,000 to R28,000 are in fact coloureds and Asians. Dennis Etheridge, Executive Director of Anglo-American, painted a portrait of the black employee at the lower fringe of the job market. 'He has a primary education at best; he is a migrant, having left his family behind, or an urban dweller in crowded conditions;

Third, and perhaps most significant, apartheid legislation, which still determines the foundation of the state despite Riekert and Wiehahn, smothers much of the social differentiation that might be expected to develop with the growth of the economy. Africans who achieve a higher income level do not necessarily turn away from the many poor, if only because both are black and, therefore, discriminated against. Or, if they do try and distance themselves, as constituting a new class of wealth and opportunity, there is nowhere for them to go. They cannot cross the racial divide. The dilemma is set out by A.J. Koornhof in his interesting study of Soweto.[27] The following extract is long but illuminating:

> Through the findings of the survey, the emergence of a well-educated, well-off elite group of Sowetans became apparent . . . The accommodation and advancement of such an urban African middle-class group is in concurrence with central government policy, and the middle class is expected to be a stabilizing force in African townships . . . The Soweto middle-class respondents reacted quite differently, however, to what was predicted . . . The fact that they were better-off and had more privileges did not change their attitudes towards people of different classes. The middle-class group continued to identify with the fate of their less well-off and less-privileged compatriots . . . Even if a middle-class group were slowly alienated from the African workers class, as well as the liberation movements, the grounds for associating with members of the white middle classes would be blocked by the predominance of segregatory institutions.
>
> The urban African middle class perceived differentiation in income and education more in terms of injustices perpetuated by the system than in terms of their own advancement in society . . . The most important differentiation experienced by all Sowetans is that of race, which in South African society tends to overshadow all other differentiations which may exist.

The contradiction between economics and politics is plain. The

his career opportunities are *severely* limited; he is not free to move in the labour market; he will meet conflicting cultural values in an English or Afrikaans environment although neither is his home language; and he will not be paid enough to be sure that his family is properly housed and fed.'

former pushes for change, whereas politicians oppose any further concessions, particularly those affecting the Group Areas Act, influx control and the pass laws. South Africa is beginning to be an advanced industrial society which needs to become sophisticated – computerized, automated, with improved communications at every level within an open, decentralized economy – but it is also a tightly regulated and controlled society under party bosses. If the analogy were not so absurd, one might draw the parallel between South Africa and the Soviet Union in the combination of political repression and the striving for modernization. It is, in fact, an extraordinarily difficult problem. How do authoritarian regimes which control industrial economies move towards liberalization? The argument is also one of tomorrow versus today. The business world holds out the prospect of greater wealth for the whole of South Africa, but the political fears that stand in the way of its realization are immediate. Despite the minority of voters who support the PFP and its call for fundamental reform, the evidence of successive elections is that the majority is not prepared to surrender control. And the effect is clear. The National Party leaders reflect the deep-seated fears of those from whom they draw support. They are constrained, therefore, by what they believe to be the limits to political action.

C. Social policy

A government intent on ending apartheid would need to encourage the reformation of society along lines of social rather than racial differentiation, using the wealth of a mining/industrial economy to move away from inequality. It might not get very far – only so far, say, as Brazil. Very probably, the social divisions of wealth and status would still correspond in broad terms with those of colour, but such a society would be without the rigidity of racial laws, and it would be moderated by a single South African patriotism through the incorporation of all its citizens into the framework of a national community. It is a direction in which the Western powers are anxious to prod South Africa. Look at the advantages, they say: a rational society without the irrationality of racist laws, a state free of the opprobrium that apartheid brings to white South Africa, a republic whose economy could use its vast hinterland to full advantage, and in which international capital would be eager to invest. It might not be quite as democratic as one would like — it might even be like Brazil — but South Africa today is only a mockery of democracy, whereas change in the direction of an open society — a national electorate and a respectable place within the international world — would surely bring immense advantages.

Well, perhaps, but to whom? Some might gain, but who might lose? Before attempting an answer, we should note a more modest version of a South Africa able to reform without revolution. It, too, emphasizes the need to look at the economics of change, and at the growing network of interests between the different communities. The argument runs as follows. The encouragement of common standards in 'own affairs', together with the erosion of restrictive policies, will one day prove to be not the winding-sheet of a dying society but the fabric of a new republic. There are already, it is said, a number of hopeful indicators. Wage rates in the newer industries — the growth points of South African enterprises — are beginning to be determined by skill not race; job reservation, following the Riekert Report, is almost an anachronism; and influx controls will have to be relaxed as labour shortages get worse. A generally healthy sign is the retreat of government from too direct an intervention in the economy. The market place is being left to market forces, and the future role of central administration ought to be, indeed must surely be, the attempt to reach common standards of rewards and benefits across the 'ethnic divide', while coopting leaders to serve on public corporations, state commissions, administrative bodies and, in time, political councils. Nor should the new constitution be taken too literally. The absurdity of a tricameral legislature will evolve into a single chamber, and the President's Council (or some other instrument of control) will draw together representatives of Africans as well as the minority communities in some new form of consultative body. At worst, the state will exercise a repressive tolerance — stick and carrot — by which it will set boundaries to what it will allow politically and economically and socially. At best, it will be the guardian of a plural society whose members, bound by mutual interests, will have too much to lose to want to put their future at risk.

Professor Leonard Thompson of Yale, drawing on writings by Heribert Adam and Hermann Giliomee, spelled out the future. He thought that 'South Africa differed so profoundly from a primary colonial situation that the racial line would eventually be superseded by cross-cutting alliances, and the black middle classes would perceive themselves as beneficiaries of a modified and stabilized, but not revolutionized, society.'[28] Such is also the vision of the true *verligte* (reformist) within the Anglo-Afrikaner community.

There are immense difficulties about accepting such arguments, whether in favour of a Brazilian policy, or as a reasoned defence of incremental change. The immediate problem in 1984 was the actual sequence of events. Throughout the closing months of the year the *Cape Argus* and the (Johannesburg) *Star* were full of the anger of black townships, including school boycotts, the burning of public buildings and the murder of frightened black councillors – frightened, one must add, by the rage of those whom they hoped to represent. What had happened to cooption? After the murder of officials in Sharpeville and neighbouring townships, authority within the black urban councils crumbled away. Mayors and councillors resigned: nobody wanted to be elected or appointed in their place. Mr Kebani Moloi (Mayor of Duduze within the Vaal triangle) was reported as saying: 'I find we are faced with government officials who want to implement apartheid, and whatever representations we make just fall flat. We try very hard to present the feelings of residents but government officials won't listen.'[29] Control reverted to Administrative Boards, and the government forgot its role as reformer. It turned to sections 28 and 29 of the Internal Security Act, detaining in prison without trial a number of leading trade-unionists;[30] it sent 7,000 soldiers and police into the township at Sebokeng; it dismissed 6,000 Sasol workers who had joined a two-day stoppage of work (5 and 6 November); and it used force against mass protests, until the number of dead and injured across the country exceeded those at Sharpeville in 1960 or Soweto in 1976. What likelihood, therefore, is there of any common ground for black and white interests?

Perhaps that is too immediate a view. Violence in the townships comes and goes, since it is in the nature of such eruptions to flare up and then become quiescent. But, assuming that the government still decides to move towards reform and away from the inequalities described earlier, can it reallocate resources to achieve a fairer society? The question is not only whether the political will to do so is there, but what price will be asked of those who must lose that others may gain. In brief, what freedom of action does Mr Botha in practice possess?

Very little, if recent research is valid. There is no dispute about in-equalities between whites and non-whites in relation to provision for education or health or social services. Since whites, who constitute less than a fifth of the population, receive a disproportionate share of total incomes, one might suppose that the state would tilt the balance towards the black majority through the provision of services: but, of course, that is not how South African society works. In practice, in 1982-3, the government spent $913 per head on schooling for whites, $258 for coloureds, and $140 for Africans. (Moreover, some 60 per cent of black teachers were unqualified, compared with only 3 per cent of white teachers.) Housing provision for blacks is dismal. Medical facilities are little better. Only 5.5 per cent of South Africa's doctors practise in the rural areas, where, after all, almost 50 per cent of the population lives. The position in the national states is even more desperate; one doctor to 174,000.[31] State pensions and other forms of social security scarcely exist for the African population.

Now consider the figures examined by Mr Charles Simkins in his submissions to the Carnegie study. Mr Simkins calculated the costs involved in bringing standards of education and health towards an equality of service for all races over the next quarter of a century and found that, even assuming a high level of economic growth and generous budgeting, there would have to be a substantial lowering of benefits for whites: 'Equalization would mean a small rise in standards for non-whites and a fall of 28 per cent for whites' by the year 2000.

When one looks at likely economic and population growth rates, one finds that the tendencies to redistribute state welfare expenditure towards the poorer population groups will be operating within modest and possibly very slender margins of growth. *Per capita* state welfare expenditure on whites will have to drop, and those on coloureds and Indians may do little more than remain static. This will make the political struggle on fiscal issues intense.[32]

That will surely be true, and there is always the terrible weight of numbers — 11 *million* Africans in the Republic, and a further 11 *million* in the national states, for whom the government in Pretoria cannot in reality wash its hands of all responsibility.

There must be great doubt, therefore, whether the government has any room for manoeuvre. One must note, too, that the figures quoted by Mr Simkins are on the basis of a reasonable, even an optimistic, estimate of economic growth. And for the immediate future the prospects are far from good. The economy is in poor shape — a falling gold price, rising inflation, heavy defence expenditure and high costs of production. The government is stretched almost beyond its means, spending not only what it has, but what it has yet to raise in taxation from a largely white electorate. It is overstretched by promises that are critical to its 'total strategy of control'. It must deliver some material reward for its new coloured and Indian voters; it cannot shed all responsibility for the national states; it is committed, as we shall see, to underpinning the Nkomati Accords; it must keep up its guard in Namibia and along its other borders. It is also beholden — fully beholden — to its loyalist following: hence the substantial increase in salaries and emoluments to civil servants and party officials within that central core of political support on which its rule depends.

If, in practical terms, the room for reform is narrow, what can one say of the *willingness* to change? Can the European minority accept the argument that fundamental reform, including an overall drop in living standards, is the price it must pay? Perhaps there is a greater generosity (mixed with fear) than is acknowledged? Perhaps the electorate has yet to be asked the right questions, or to be offered the principled leadership that might persuade it to accept reform? To be asked whether one is willing to accept majority rule is one form of interrogation: to have put before one some such question as 'Do you believe that voting should be irrespective of race?' might elicit a different response. The problem, however, is the National Party, for it is difficult to believe that any section of the African population would agree to accommodate its interests to the requirements of the leadership of the party. Compromise would require a new Afrikaner leader, or a shift away from the bureaucratic/security emphasis of the inner core of party members, and the prospect of such a change is slight. In brief, to ask the present leadership of the National Party to move substantial resources and political rights away from the white minority is to ask more than its own history can provide. For there is always the alternative of coercion. The old Adam of repression has been quick to assert itself against the new Adam of reform. Look at the events of 1983–4. At the first sign of opposition during elections for the new constitution – in itself a limited reform – the government did not seek consensus but obedience. It turned instinctively to the controlling power of the state, not to the deliberative machinery of parliament. Politics in white South Africa follows its own *daimon* and listens primarily to the emotions and fears of the past.

One last example of the inability of Mr Botha's government to escape from that past. Among the reforms offered to the business world in 1984 was the abolition of the 'coloured labour preference quota' in the Western Cape. Designed to protect coloured workers against African competition, the quota was often evaded – the settlements of black labour at Crossroads, Langa, Nyanga and Guguletu are ample testimony to the constant influx of migrants from the Transkei, Ciskei and the Eastern Cape – and its abolition was a sensible measure, since the economy of the region requires all the labour it can get. Even more sensible would have been the lifting of the pass laws and restrictions on residence for blacks and coloureds. That would indeed have been reform. Even as an interim measure, however, the government might usefully have set about renovating the older delapidated African settlements while providing adequate facilities for the 80,000 or more squatters at Crossroads. Instead it is building Khayelitsha.

Khayelitsha is a new, large, sand- and windswept settlement for black workers. It is sited on the barren coast of the Cape Peninsula. 'The township is colourless, regimented and remote, bordered on two sides by Defence Force property and on a third by the sea. Even on a slightly windy day residents breath sand, and the children play in it and house-wives wage a constant war against it.'[33] It is bleak, and it is the government's solution to the illegal African settlement of Crossroads. It represents everything that brings the government into conflict with blacks, not only by what it does but over suspicion of what it intends to do. At Khayelitsha the accusation is that the administration cannot bring itself to do what is necessary, namely, make provision for a permanent, reasonably placed, reasonably housed African community within easy reach of employment. The Riekert and Wiehahn Commissions examined the problem, the business community emphasizes the need to improve labour costs, politicians know that inadequate housing, high transport costs and lack of social amenities are the prime cause of the violence which tears at South African society, and the government produces Khayelitsha.

It is forty kilometres from Cape Town, and workers on R10 a day pay up to R3 daily for travel. There are now 15,000 'core houses' — that is, metal huts — packed in rows under the high-mast lighting common to African townships. It is, to put the matter neutrally, bleak. But of course conditions are always relative and the government can point to advantages: piped water, sewerage, schools, subsidized rents and a 99-year leasehold. It is at this point, however, that suspicion begins to surface. The rent is subsidized at R20 a month, but why? The government has also agreed that not only legally employed Africans but 'illegals' can move to Khayelitsha, although Dr Gerrit Wiljoen, minister of cooperation, announced that they would only be allowed to live in shacks within the serviced township and 'would not qualify for urban residence'. And again the question is asked, why should that be so?

The obvious reason is the wish to remove the squatters at Crossroads. It is part of the endless removal of black people — by persuasion if possible (subsidized rent) and by force if necessary (police dogs, magistrates and bulldozers). Other fears arise. The government wants to demolish Crossroads, but does it also intend to move all black residents in the Western Cape, legal and illegal, into Khayelitsha, where they will be under strict control, clearing families out of the earlier settlements in favour perhaps of coloureds rather than Africans? If not, why is there a freeze on house improvements in the older areas, large rent increases and no leasehold? And will women and children continue to be deported to KwaZulu or the Ciskei where tribal chiefs act as surrogate magistrates for white South Africa, while only the 'skilled black male' is allowed to live and work in the Cape?[34]

Nobody knows, and the uncertainty itself robs the government of what little belief there is in its good intentions. It shifts between promising reform and being incapable of reform. It was suggested at the beginning of the chapter that a proper comparison for the 1980s was the 1960s, in the sense that the Botha administration wants to move the country away from 'dogmatic apartheid'. Perhaps it has a little, but in doing so it has also lost something of the assurance of control that Verwoerd exhibited. The post-Soweto years have not been like the post-Sharpeville years. The government reacts more than it directs, and gives the appearance in domestic policy of floundering amidst events which it can neither foresee nor control. The Sorcerer's Apprentice no longer knows what to do. And were a future administration to try to undo more of the past, would it be any better placed to meet the needs of an industrial society in which non-white skills and purchasing power are basic to its wealth? The economy calls for measures that politicians will not introduce; the minimal reforms sanctioned by government fall short of what is urgently needed. Meanwhile the African majority, which rightly sees that political power is the key to economic gain and full status within the Republic, continues to be excluded from a constitution designed to bolster the European minority. Little wonder, therefore, that the prevailing mood is one of protest and uncertainty.

3 Pax Pretoriana

'Thy wars brought nothing about;
Thy lovers were all untrue.'
(John Dryden, *The Secular Masque*)

If in its internal affairs the government has run out of reforms, that does not seem to be the case abroad. The record of its success might be thought striking. It has bought time, sealed its borders, reduced its neighbours to clients and staved off in Namibia a settlement on terms urged by the United Nations. It has survived the withdrawal of colonial power, thrown back the challenge of armed African states and reduced to something close to surrender the threat of Marxist governments on its borders.

The change in fortune is remarkable. In 1980 South Africa appeared under siege. The former barrier of colonial and settler-ruled states was down; there were safe havens for ANC guerrillas. The comparison was with Vietnam — a militant communism backed by the Soviet Union, pressing down on a minority regime which was already challenged within its own borders. Soweto, Angola, Mozambique, SWAPO, the Cubans, the front-line states: surely, it was argued, battle must soon be joined. No one draws such parallels today. The image presented by Pretoria is very different. It is that of an aggressive, anti-communist, dominant power. Success has heightened the rhetoric: South Africa is a regional superpower, southern Africa a subcontinent. The position of white South Africa is no longer that of Israel, a beleaguered state, but of the United States in, say, the Caribbean, a protective power which keeps at bay external forces (Cuba, the USSR) that threaten the region.

Peace, therefore, throughout the subcontinent, may be enforced once Namibia is settled. The lion will lie down with the lamb, South Africa will guard o'er the fold. The image often used by the National Party is of the starry sky. The half-dozen governments of the region, it is said, form a constellation of states, each protective of its neighbours, each profiting from the collective strength of their number. Sometimes the imagery is changed a little. Officials in Pretoria now talk of a planetary system in which the Republic exerts a gravitational pull on a number of lesser worlds: an inner ring of satellites, Lesotho, Botswana, Swaziland; an outer ring, Mozambique, Zimbabwe, Namibia; and, further off, the republics of Malawi, Zambia and Angola. Such terminology corresponds with South Africa's internal system of dependence: the core population of Afrikaners plus fellow Europeans, and the lesser worlds of coloureds, Indians, national states and black townships. A vision of peace and plenty under a Pax Pretoriana.

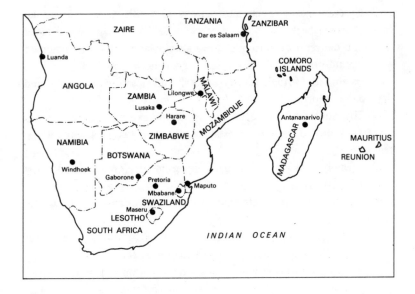

Southern Africa, including Angola, Zimbabwe and Mozambique: i.e., the 'constellation of states'.

How has it been brought about? By imposing friendship through military strength and economic power. South Africa's neighbours are under African leaders who talk loudly but carry no stick. They are troubled by local dissidents and, Zimbabwe apart, have very little power to deal with them — UNITA in Angola, a resistance movement in Mozambique, a Liberation Army in Lesotho. One can also add unrest in Matabeleland in Zimbabwe. There are levers, therefore, that Pretoria can use against those who reject its help. In the early 1980s, South Africa became a predatory state whose neighbours felt its power to their cost. Its troops invaded Angola to do battle with the Cubans; they entered Maputo and Maseru to attack ANC/PAC bases. The government threatened economic sanctions against Zimbabwe — a true reversal of roles — by withholding essential rolling-stock from the Harare/Johannesburg rail network. It supported Savimbi in Angola and local bandits in Mozambique. That was the dark side of reprisals and intimidation. But South Africa also began to offer food, technical help, economic assistance and mutual defence arrangements under an umbrella of regional security.

The advantages of such negotiations to South Africa are easy to catalogue:

1. The danger to the Republic has always been the combination of external and domestic threats — sabotage at home supplied from ANC enclaves abroad. Mutual security pacts should close such bolt-holes and dry up the supply.

2. The South African economy needs to expand, and a friendly hinterland should help to re-establish the political economy of the region.

3. Friendly relations with black governments (even black Marxist governments) bring a good deal of satisfaction, since they enable the National Party to justify its claim to be the guardian of order within the region.

4. Nothing is more likely to soften American and European attitudes towards South Africa than success as a stabilizing force.

5. Recognition of South African strength, not only in military terms but politically and economically, weakens attempts such as the Southern African Development Coordination Conference (SADCC) to isolate South Africa.[35]

6. Mutual defence pacts lighten the burden on the Republic's defence budget and reduce public disquiet over casualties in the border wars.

7. Lastly, peace and goodwill abroad have a doubly beneficial effect on internal order. Friends are uplifted, enemies discouraged. Terrorists can be defeated at home because they lack support abroad.

They lack support abroad because of the preoccupation of organizations and countries which profess to be the allies of South Africa's enemies. The OAU is divided, the Soviet Union is elsewhere engaged. The case hardly needs proving.

The Organization of African Unity is a sorry spectacle today. It mirrors the plight of the continent it tries to represent. Appropriately sited in the capital of a country devastated by war and famine, the OAU is no longer capable of mobilizing African support in defence of African interests. It cannot negotiate successfully in Chad or the western Sahara; it can scarcely meet without division. (Its principal contribution to South African liberation is through the ANC's broadcasts from Addis Ababa.) Many of its members now face domestic problems and border quarrels which leave them no time for larger issues. It is also ideologically in disarray, since it now has among its signatory states governments in Mozambique and Swaziland which are in treaty relationship with South Africa.

The Russians, too, are distracted, under new conservative leaders. Moscow might perhaps have persuaded Mozambique not to sign at Nkomati had it been able to offer an equivalent measure of assistance, including full membership of the CMEA and sufficient military force to deter South Africa. It could, or would, not do so. Superpower is valid only against superpower. The USSR's interests are stretched across the world in Vietnam, Poland, Cuba, Afghanistan, South Yemen and Ethiopia. Its economy is in no condition to take on extra burdens. Its military preoccupations are elsewhere, and it now seems likely that it will see the Marxist regimes in Maputo and Luanda (which had hoped to depend on it) drift away. The Cubans, too, are overcommitted in both Angola and Ethiopia. Moscow and Havana are distant from Maputo, Pretoria is close; and President Machel went where help was forthcoming.

Nkomati, 1984

'Solitudinem faciunt, pacem appellant.' The full title of the treaty speaks for itself: 'An agreement on non-aggression and good neighbour-liness between the government of the People's Republic of Mozambique and the government of the Republic of South Africa'. It reaffirms the principle of non-interference in the internal affairs of other states and spells out the terms of non-interference. A large part of the text consists of plaintive attempts by Mozambique to insist on abstract principles, and of precise statements by South Africa of its needs. The treaty is said to rest on 'the internationally recognized principle of the right of peoples to self-determination and independence and the principle of equal rights of all peoples'. *But* 'the High Contracting Parties shall not allow their respective territories . . . to be used as a base . . . by organiz-ations or individuals which plan or prepare to commit acts of violence and terrorism'.

In theory there were mutual advantages to be had. Mozambique had been invaded by South African forces. Its territory was awash with dis-sident bands of mercenaries and aggrieved minorities, whose leaders, grouped loosely as the Mozambique National Resistance (MNR), had been armed and financed by South Africa and clandestine sources abroad. Therefore, 'the High Contracting Parties forbid and prevent in their respective territories the organization of irregular forces or armed bands, including mercenaries . . . They undertake not to resort, individ-ually or collectively, to the threat or use of force against each other's sovereignty, territorial integrity or political independence.'

South Africa, on the other hand, wanted to seal its borders against the ANC: 'The High Contracting Parties undertake to eliminate from their respective territories bases, training centres, places for shelter, accommodation and transit for [terrorists] .'

The treaty establishes a Joint Standing Committee to 'monitor the application' of the agreements reached between Machel and Botha. The two leaders affirmed their understanding of each other to such a degree that one rubs one's eyes in disbelief. Was it really the white Afrikaner and the black Marxist who so much admired each other?

In his speech welcoming the treaty (printed together with the text), Marshal Samora Moises Machel blamed the past — that poor scapegoat of Third World leaders: 'We are laying the foundations for a definitive break of the cycle of violence . . . that was above all the result of the burden of legacies we carry with us. A violence that began some centuries ago when the dignity and personality of African peoples were trampled on by the aggression, domination and exploitation of European colonialism.'

Part of Machel's speech was taken up with (exculpatory?) praise of the OAU, 'under its galaxy of illustrious leaders who had the lucidity . . . to give form to the aspiration of unity so that the struggle of the African people for the liberation of the continent could continue'. He noted the principle, too, that 'there is peace only when life, liberty and the dignity of man is respected without any discrimination'. For the rest, the words declaimed by Machel must have been music to Afrikaner ears:

> None of us, Mozambicans or South Africans, have another country. We are not foreigners to our continent . . . Our states have been able to map out the path of coexistence . . . Many have been surprised at the speed with which we found the answers without external assistance . . . It enables the region to concentrate its efforts on the prime struggle of the continent and humanity − the struggle against hunger, disease, ignorance, poverty and underdevelopment − a *luta continua*.

Mr Botha matched his eloquence. He, too, came from among the victims of imperialism: 'South Africa was one of the first countries of Africa to confront colonial occupation and foreign occupation . . . Our independence did not come easily. Countless numbers of our women and children died in concentration camps while their husbands, fathers and brothers fought the might of a great empire.'

All that was in the past. Now they were free. Moreover, South Africa had

> The stability, the economic strength and the productive capacity to assist its neighbours in achieving the regional goal of progress and development, provided the countries concerned were prepared to seek healthier mutual relations. My country offered to sign non-aggression pacts with all its neighbours in pursuit of that objective, and today with the People's Republic of Mozambique we are taking an important step in that direction.

I see a subcontinent in which countries work together, increase production, develop regional trade . . . and programmes to overcome drought, floods and other natural disasters . . . A veritable constellation of states working together on the basis of mutual respect.

It was a remarkable mixture of sentiment and reality, but the triumph was surely Botha's. In close up, we can see the pressure that South Africa exerted on a destitute economy. Although there is a spread of interests between the two countries, the balance is always on the side of the white republic. In labour migration, a tradition going back to the nineteenth century, the numbers entering South Africa from Mozambique total some 50,000. They work in the mines and on farms in the lowveld. Still today, as under the Portuguese, mineworkers receive their wages through a deferred payment scheme whereby the Mozambique government gets some R90 million in foreign exchange, then hands on payments in local currency. Trade is heavily in South Africa's favour — exports of R160 million, imports of only R14 million — despite payments for electricity from Cabora Bassa. The importance of Mozambique to South Africa is the proximity of Maputo, where the harbour authorities can handle a substantial proportion of South Africa's exports. Hence the presence of South African engineers and administrators in the capital of the Marxist republic. There were reasons enough at the beginning of 1984 why Pretoria should prefer peace to war, but they were not of the order of magnitude that weighed upon Maputo.[36] It was the near collapse of the Mozambique state, its inability to put down those in rebellion against it, and its lack of basic foods which brought Machel to Nkomati.

There is a residual problem for Pretoria. Success has produced its own difficulties. By 1984 the economy of Mozambique was devastated, the state was broken-backed. It was not quite the outcome South Africa wanted, since it has no wish to underpin the economy of bankrupt states. Moreover, it needs Mozambique labour, and it depends on Maputo as a working port. The problem, therefore, is to strike a balance between means and ends, destruction and dependence, keeping Frelimo under pressure from the MNR, which South Africa can neither fully control nor fully suppress, without reducing the country to an unworkable economy. Whether, in fact, South Africa still looks for the overthrow of Machel, or whether it believes he is now a tamed, reliable neighbour, remains in doubt. Perhaps the National Party itself is undecided?

In brief, it is possible today to hold three different views of the treaty:

1. *Mutual advantage.* It enabled Mozambique to survive. South Africa was in danger of playing Israel to its neighbouring territories, ending in the misery of a divided Lebanon. Botha avoided that, Machel avoided that.

2. *South Africa miscalculated.* By enabling Machel to survive, it failed to eliminate the future threat of a Marxist state. It was in these terms that Machel announced the 'victory' of Nkomati.

3. *Mozambique miscalculated.* By submitting to Pretoria, Machel failed to understand that Botha would not control the MNR. Because Botha had been minister of defence, Machel thought that Botha, Magnus Malan and Pik Botha could ensure his safety: he underestimated the extent of South Africa's malevolence.

At the end of 1984 aspects of all three views were evident, but it would be an unwise observer who came down strongly in favour of any one of the three. The treaty itself was certainly the most dramatic illustration of a general pattern and it is bound to be looked at closely by other governments. It also showed how greatly the tide of events since 1974 has turned in South Africa's favour. The anxieties once expressed in Pretoria over the collapse of Portuguese rule have given way to satisfaction, and one ought not to be surprised. The apparent shift in policy from destabilization to offers of collaboration is simply the turning of the same coin of diplomacy. When South African leaders are threatened, they react aggressively; when the enemy is seen as a paper tiger, its whiskers and tail are tweaked. Very likely the strength of South Africa was always bound to assert itself, and the fact that neighbours have settled for peace rather than force is no more than a reflection of the underlying disparities of power.

That was always true of the three countries whose governments have had to sup with the devil. Swaziland, Lesotho and Botswana only narrowly escaped being handed over to the Republic — there was provision for their transfer under the 1910 Act of Union — until the tide of emancipation carried all three into a dependent sovereignty in the 1960s: they are still within the South African monetary and customs union under an agreed formula for the transfer of revenue from Pretoria to Maseru, Gaborone and Mbabane. It is wrong, however, to put all three countries into one category. Swaziland has special reasons for collaboration, Lesotho goes its own way, Botswana maintains a careful, and one should add democratic, distance from Pretoria.

Swaziland

Relations with South Africa are a complicated tale of promise and non-fulfilment. The story begins in late 1981, early 1982, when a treaty was hatched between Pretoria and King Sobhuza (who died shortly after-wards), the terms of which were made public by Dr Piet Koornhof, minister of cooperation and development, in a speech to the KwaZulu Legislative Assembly on 14 June 1982. There was to be a transfer of territory to Swaziland:[37] 'To finalize the border adjustment, it will be necessary to excise the Ingwavuma district from the area of jurisdiction of the KwaZulu government. Similarly the KaNgwane Legislative Assembly and Executive Council will be dissolved . . . and the national state of KaNgwane absorbed into Swaziland.'

There was an immediate uproar. Mr Mabuza, leader of the Inyandza movement in KaNgwane, was understandably upset. Chief Buthelezi was incensed. 'If we had guns, you would not dare to do it, but because you have guns and we have no guns, you can do it.' The transfer meant that some one million Swazi-speaking people would be transferred from the Republic to Swaziland, giving the landlocked kingdom access to the sea south of Mozambique. Buthelezi took the issue to the Natal Supreme Court, which judged that the government had acted contrary to the National States Constitution Act of 1971. The government appealed, lost, took the case to the Appellate Court in Bloemfontein, and lost again. After some hesitation, and after appointing the Rumpff Commission to re-examine the problem, the government accepted the court's findings and dissolved the commission.

The dilemma was clear. As Chief Buthelezi noted: 'When Proclamation 121 was published as a step towards handing over KaNgwane and Ingwavuma to Swaziland, a secret non-aggression pact and treaty with Swaziland had already been concluded. Quite clearly, the cession of KaNgwane and the district of Ingwavuma was the pay-off to Swaziland for having entered into the pact in secret.'

In fact, Swaziland kept its side of the bargain. It 'clamped down severely on the activities of the ANC Mission in exile and deported hundreds of members from its territory'. South Africa could take comfort, therefore, in having closed a sanctuary of ANC support in a country whose border with Mozambique is almost as long as that with the Republic itself.

Lesotho

Migrant labour is drawn from the small mountainous kingdom into South Africa's mines, and Lesotho is entirely dependent on its powerful neighbour. Neither the King, nor Chief Jonathan and his National Party government, is easily controlled. There is a waywardness of behaviour that served Lesotho well enough in the long struggle to avoid Boer domination a century ago. Nevertheless, South Africa can threaten to support Jonathan's enemies in exile – particularly the Democratic Party and the Lesotho Liberation Army, whose local guerrillas find refuge among villages in the Maluti mountains – and in recent years troubles have come not as single spies but in battalions. In June 1982, the Lesotho minister of works was assassinated. The following December, the South African Defence Force crossed the border into Maseru in search of ANC members and, in the attack, over 40 men, women and children were killed.

Today, relations between Pretoria and Maseru are less strained. The South African government has arrested members of the Liberation Army, and Chief Jonathan has expelled ANC members from his capital. There is a see-saw relationship, however, between the two. Lesotho has lived long enough with South Africa to know the limits of defiance: Pretoria can intimidate, but it cannot yet bring Jonathan to sign an 'Nkomati' pact.

Botswana

The Democratic Party government under President Quett Masire has been an even less biddable neighbour. It has kept Pretoria at arm's length. Mr Archie Mogwe (the foreign minister who lost his seat in parliament in the September 1984 elections) observed that 'the South

African government, which is at war with its own people, wants Botswana to do what it cannot do itself. With all its military might, even South Africa cannot stop its enemies getting through to Johannesburg or Durban.' The Nkomati Treaty was forced on Mozambique, and a similar agreement was sought from Botswana. 'The deal was concluded with Mozambique in order to isolate and compartmentalize one country after another in this region along the lines of the so-called homelands'; but, said Mogwe, 'we are not so dumb as to allow the ANC or any other anti-South African body to use our territory. We do not want to be placed in the position of also having to sign a non-aggression pact.'[38]

Botswana has been troubled by border conflicts with its other neighbours, particularly Zimbabwe because of ethnic ties among the Kalanga community on both sides of the frontier who sympathize with Joshua Nkomo. Refugees from all sides have entered the country in large numbers; but, as Mr Mpuchane, High Commissioner for Botswana in London, argued:

> . . . refugees are not all terrorists. Many are fleeing oppression. We sympathize with them as human beings and we have treaty obligations to protect them. Yet this humanitarian gesture on our part is seen as a hostile act, deserving of punishment, by South Africa. In the eyes of South Africa there are no refugees, only terrorists. We have, therefore, over several years witnessed attacks on refugee settlements, and on the civilian population. We know too of the economic sabotage and blackmail aimed at keeping southern Africa beholden to South Africa.[39]

What can President Masire's government do? Very little, since 'we are still part of the customs union with South Africa and we rely heavily on the Republic for our transport and other services. There is still a food deficit in this country which requires all these facilities.'[40] All they can do is be careful, and keep their distance.

Further afield, Malawi remains resolutely on good terms with Pretoria; Dr Banda is not immortal and changes may come after his departure, but it is difficult to believe that the relationship will be substantially different. Zimbabwe, however, is a more difficult case to assess.

Zimbabwe

Robert Mugabe and his Zanu (Patriotic Front) government speak the language of rejection, denouncing Pretoria for its 'aggressive posture' and 'brazen assaults on freedom and human dignity'. There is no official recognition of South Africa. But in practice Mr Botha has little cause for exasperation. Without Mozambique's shelter of Mugabe's Zanla forces, independence might not have been won in 1980, but no such help is given by Zimbabwe to anti-South African guerrillas. The country is strategically placed in relation to the Pretoria/Witwatersand/ Vereeniging district, but no ANC or PAC officials, no camps or forces-in-training, are allowed refuge. And one can understand why there is so little heroism. There is too much to lose. Of all South Africa's neighbours, Zimbabwe comes closest to having a competitive base by reason of its financial and industrial output: but precisely on that account it needs the air, rail and road network, the power grid and consumer goods that bind its economy to the Republic. It is an inland state which must have access to the world. Hence the ambivalence about the Nkomati Treaty. It is not simply courtesy or friendship between Mugabe and Machel that prevents Harare from criticizing its terms, for if the treaty works as it should, Zimbabwe too will benefit from the cessation of guerrilla attacks within Mozambique. According to *The Times* (London) of 11 December 1984,

> The 790-mile line from Harare through Mozambique to Maputo has been closed by guerrilla sabotage since June. Traffic has instead to be sent through the northern Transvaal, crossing into Mozambique at Komatipoort, northwest of Maputo. The detour adds only 125 miles, but increases tariffs by 40 per cent, and even the short stretch of line from Komatipoort to Maputo is often cut.
>
> Even on the most optimistic prognosis, which assumes an end to the guerrilla war in Mozambique and the completion of projects to improve its port and rail system by the 9-nation Southern African Development Coordination Conference, Zimbabwe's dependence on Pretoria's transport system is never likely to drop below 30 per cent.
>
> South Africa is also likely to remain Zimbabwe's major trading partner. Attempts to stimulate trade with fellow black African states

have had little or no success, such trade accounting for no more than 10 per cent of Zimbabwe's total.

Moreover, South Africa has the power to punish. By interrupting deliveries of goods, including supplies of maize, it can make life uncomfortable for a regime unsure of itself. That it has not done so in any large measure is no guarantee that it will not do so. It can also support 'Super-Zapu' dissidents in Matabeleland, keeping the pot stirred in Zimbabwe as in Angola, Mozambique and Lesotho. There is ample evidence of its readiness to strike, and a corresponding apprehension in Harare that a South African armoured column could not be stopped and might even be welcomed all the way to Bulawayo by those who have reason to oppose the Zanu Patriotic Front government. Better, therefore, to settle for such terms as Pretoria and Harare can jointly agree. It does not have to be an Nkomati-style treaty: that might be too much to ask and too much to surrender, but an unwritten alliance that supports the *status quo* is easily seen to be in the interests of both governments.[41]

Mozambique, Lesotho, Swaziland, Botswana, Zimbabwe − the net has closed about the ANC. But one cannot truly talk of a Pax Pretoriana unless there is some kind of settlement in Namibia. The long-running conflict on South Africa's northwest border is a puzzle. Why cannot negotiations be concluded?

Namibia

The simplest explanation is that South Africa prefers an unsettled *status quo* to an agreement which admits majority rule under SWAPO, although it is not easy to see why Botha can live with Machel and not with SWAPO's leader Sam Nujoma. Perhaps the military will not let him? A more generous explanation may lie in the sheer number of those engaged in the drama. The stage is crowded with actor-managers: South Africa, SWAPO, Angola, Cuba, the Soviet Union, the United States, the Western Contact Group (USA, Britain, Canada, West Germany and until 1983 France), the African front-line states, alliances of different interests in Namibia and, of course, the UN, whose resolution 435, requiring elections, is both the trigger and the obstacle to change.* Nor do the actors stay still. They alter the script, and rewrite their demands. President Reagan, before his re-election, was looking for gains and thought that he (and his special envoy, Dr Chester Crocker) might find them in constructive engagement with South Africa, linking Cuban withdrawal from Angola with South Africa's own departure. Once he had been re-elected, the urgency grew less. The *Totentanz* of SWAPO, South Africa and local forces in Namibia and Angola is scarcely the same from one month to another.[42] There are innumerable meetings which, while not actually hovering on the brink of success, at least hold out the hope of success: meetings between South African and Angolan representatives in the Cape Verde Islands in December 1982 and February 1983, and in Paris in April 1983; further meetings in Lusaka in February 1984 between Angola, South Africa and the United States, from which came the Lusaka Agreement and a Joint Monitoring Commission, and in Lusaka again in May 1984 between the Multi-Party Conference of Namibia, Dr van Niekerk (the administrator-general in Windhoek), representatives of SWAPO and observers from Zambia.

By 1984, several delegates had changed sides: Justus Garoeb withdrew from the Damara Council, one of the many political bodies in Namibia; Nora Chase and Gerson Veii of the South West African National Union quarrelled with their president, Katjiuonga. SWAPO also picked up support from those within the European minority who were opposed to Dirk Mudge: they included the lawyer Anton Lubowski and members of the German Interessengemeinschaft. There was hostility at a personal level between Hans Diegaardt of the Rheheboth Basters and Sam Nujoma. After the Lusaka Conference in May, there was a further flurry of meetings. The Angolans talked to President Kaunda of Zambia, SWAPO went to Luanda, Toivo ja Toivo — released from prison after sixteen years on Robben Island — flew to London, Pik Botha, Magnus Malan and Dr van Niekerk journeyed to Lusaka. Señor Pérez de Cuéllar, secretary-general of the UN, met everybody, as did Chester Crocker.

Meanwhile the cost rises. A recent estimate (*Lincoln Letter*, October 1984) suggests that the actual burden on South Africa is close to twice that of the official figure of R1,143 billion. Casualties are also mounting

* The UN Assembly also recognizes SWAPO as 'the sole and legitimate representative of the peoples of Namibia'.

in the guerrilla conflict within the territory, and there are ugly stories of torture and murder — SWAPO guerrillas versus South Africa's Koevoet ('Crowbar') counter-insurgency police, helped by Kalahari bushmen-trackers. In December 1983, South African troops crossed the Namibian border into Angola and again fought a pitched battle with Cuban and FAPLA (Angolan) troops. It was only the most extravagant of several sorties. The chief sufferers, of course, are local villagers: 'As far as we are concerned, UNITA, South African, SWAPO and Angolan soldiers are the same. When they arrive we flee without asking which side they belong to.' And still the end is not in sight.

Angola

The UNITA-led guerrilla war in southern Angola is not of South Africa's making but is enormously to its advantage. In this huge, empty land of tangled bush and scattered villages, Jonas Savimbi, furnished with South African supplies, can move almost at will, and the constant threat has brought the region's second Marxist state — under the MPLA government of Eduardo dos Santos — into negotiations with Pretoria. At the end of 1984 it was forced to accept the United States formula of linkage: Cubans out of Angola, South African forces out of Namibia. In practice, neither government is prepared to endorse quite so simple an exchange. The government in Luanda needs Cuban help, if only against Savimbi, though it offered a phased departure. South Africa hesitates, and insists on immediate withdrawal. Yet as in Mozambique, its position is ambivalent. It is in favour of weakening the Marxist government; it sees no present gain in abandoning Savimbi — indeed he was invited as an official guest to Botha's inauguration — and it tries to argue the need for a coalition of MPLA and UNITA leaders. It can also pose as the protector of Western interests against Cuban/Marxist aggression. But to do that, it needs some Cubans in Angola, if only to keep up the claim. Keep the cauldron of politics and local war bubbling, therefore, provided the cost can be minimized.

It is by no means the case, then, that South Africa's wars have 'brought nothing about'. The use of force and tough negotiations have compelled recognition of its strength. It has used war and politics to reinforce its economic dominance. All road, rail and air links lead into the Republic, bringing goods and migrant labour, but the Botha government has not left the issue to market forces alone. It has imposed its will.

What it cannot achieve is a full-hearted cooperation. It is difficult to believe that any of the states which border South Africa would not oppose Pretoria if they dared to do so, just as they would, if they could, strengthen economic ties among themselves, though that too is unlikely. It is a hegemony by *force majeure* which South Africa must continue to impose. It has worked astonishingly well if one looks back to 1974. Even so, the rewards have not been quite as large as must have been hoped. The move towards Pax Pretoriana carried a double expectation. It was hoped that it would put an end to the ANC-led disturbances within the Republic by closing down its bases abroad, and that it would help to align South Africa with the West as a successful anti-communist power. Neither expectation has been fully realized. Admittedly, the ANC has been wounded — it has suffered severe setbacks — but that has not curbed unrest in South African townships or, so far as one can judge, weakened support for nationalist politics among the radical young. If only for that reason, the Western powers have been lukewarm in their support of South African diplomacy. Indeed, rioting in the Vaal triangle and the Eastern Cape, has revived anti-apartheid sentiment in Britain and the United States. There is perhaps a paradox in the actual measure of South Africa's success. The more it seals its frontiers along the great arc of territory from Maputo to Luanda, the more pressure it generates within its own borders. Governments, observed Hegel, frequently engage in wars abroad in order to ensure domestic tranquillity; South Africa's wars have failed to achieve domestic peace. And that, in turn, casts doubt on the permanence of Pretoria's success.

4 A conflict of policies

Do nothing, or do something? The case for moderate inaction is attractive. It is time, one can argue, to shake off the guilt that has confused Western policy. Because white South Africans are of European origin, that does not make them our responsibility. The Germans behaved worse in the 1930s, the Americans were no better a generation ago in Alabama, Georgia, Mississippi; and because South Africans behave as badly today as we did yesterday, that does not make us accomplices. It may be that many of us would act no better if we were similarly placed: the evidence from Kenya and Rhodesia is suggestive. But we are not similarly placed and, in relation to South Africa, we have no particular grounds for condemnation or exculpation. We certainly have no special insight into its mismanagement or remedy for its cure. It was the over-simple proposition entertained recently by President Carter, and by Mr Jesse Jackson today, that South Africa should be led marching through Georgia in the wake of desegregation in the United States. We like to interpret the world in our image, and South Africa is seen by many Americans as a kind of misguided southern state, just as some British observers still see the Republic as a lapsed Commonwealth member. But the parallels are not close. There is no federal government to enforce judgments on the South African government, as the Supreme Court in Washington once enforced decisions on Alabama and Arkansas. Apartheid is the policy of a sovereign state. It is true that the regime in Pretoria is odious. So are many others. It is also an affront to coloured peoples throughout the world, but the evils listed without regard to race, religion or ideology in the registers of Amnesty International are an affront to humanity itself. What difference does it make to the prisoner who screams out in pain whether his gaoler is white, black, communist, fascist or nationalist? There are more deaths in police custody, more torture under political oppression, in many Latin American states than in South Africa; there are Commonwealth countries in which society is more brutish and governments more brutal, unable to impose any ordered framework of control, although they may lack the endurance of National Party rule. The grounds may seem ample, therefore, for treating the Republic as simply one among the world's many oppressive states.

Common sense adds weight to the side of doing very little. No one has any belief today in the power of sanctions to bring about more than marginal change. It was not economic sanctions but guerrilla war, and the sanctuary afforded to Mugabe's Zanla forces, which brought the downfall of white rule in Zimbabwe — that, and the residual authority of the former colonial power. And suppose sanctions were imposed against South Africa? At what point would the Western powers have to intervene, either to ensure their success or to restore order? And at what cost? A blockade? . . . followed by fighting? . . . followed by an occupying force? . . . followed by international tension over who should rule in Pretoria? Who would benefit? Not, surely, the citizens of South Africa, certainly not in the short run. To impose sanctions and then see them fail, or stretch out over years of international argument, would be foolish; but to bring about the collapse of an economy that still manages — however unfairly — to feed, clothe, shelter and reward its inhabitants cannot be in the interests of any Western trading nation, still less of South Africa's already stricken neighbours.

And why risk the destruction of what is vital to many Western societies? The economic importance of South Africa hardly needs stressing. It furnishes essential raw materials, provides employment and adds to the trading wealth of the industrial world. The point is well made by Professor Arnt Spandau: 'As a gold-producing and capital-importing country, South Africa is an exceptionally valuable trading partner. The value of its merchandise imports exceeds the value of exports by a wide margin. As a result, its manufactured goods do not come into full competition . . . because South Africa finances her trade deficit by the sale of newly mined gold and other materials.'[43]

In recent years, South African manufacturers have displaced some (British) goods in Malawi and Zimbabwe, but in general terms the argument holds good. The figures shown in Tables 3 and 4 cannot be

Table 3 Current account balance, 1982 (R million)

Merchandise — exports. f.o.b.	10,132
Gold output	8,627
Service receipts	3,612
Merchandise — imports. f.o.b.	(—) 18,099
Services	(—) 7,648
Transfers	339
Balance on current account:	(—) 3,037

Source: South African Reserve Bank, *Quarterly Bulletin*, March 1983, quoted by Spandau, *Southern Africa and the Western World.*

Table 4 Direction of trade, 1983 (US $ million)

	Exports to RSA	Imports from RSA	Balance for OECD country
UK	1,687	1,255	(+) 432
USA	2,132	2,028	(+) 104
FRG	1,946	874	(+) 1,072
Japan	1,742	1,619	(+) 123

Source: OECD, *Monthly Statistics of Foreign Trade*, January 1985.

blinked away. South Africa disturbs the conscience of Western nations, but it also lines their pockets. As for their imports from South Africa, it was not the West but Providence which placed so much mineral wealth within a limited area of the world, a parallel to that other source of manna from the underworld in the countries of Arabia. Moreover, by an ironic turn of fate, any interruption of supply would shift the Western powers' dependence for many of their minerals from the Republic to the Soviet Union. At the end of the nineteenth century, South Africa drew the capitalist world of finance and adventurers to its mining economy — ruffians who grew rich on gold and diamonds until they settled to a respectable life in multinational companies and corporate finance. The list of vital minerals today — vital either strategically (platinum, cobalt, manganese, chromium) or commercially (gold, silver, diamonds, nickel, copper, uranium, vanadium, lead, zinc, coal, tin, ferrous metals) — is very long. They are the sinews of the modern world and its industrial societies.[44]

The pattern of South African trade and investment has been unusually consistent. Over 60 per cent of its imports, and over 50 per cent of its exports other than gold, are consigned to four industrial countries – Britain, the United States, West Germany and Japan. It has been so for many years. Capital movements have changed a little. There is more indirect, less direct, investment by both Britain and the United States, and a large part of the 'new capital' is reinvestment from subsidiaries based in the Republic. There have also been brief periods of alarm, post-Sharpeville, post-Soweto, but the element of risk is more than offset by the rate of return. The scale of South African investment abroad has also grown, particularly in Zimbabwe: hence the unspoken relationship between Pretoria and Harare?

For many years, Britain was the dominant purchaser, just as it was the chief supplier and investor, and the legacy is still there: £3,790 million of trade, £11 billion invested (direct investment, £5,000 million; portfolio stock, £6,000 million). The value can be matched by adding trade and investment returns from African countries, particularly Nigeria, but that simply brings the argument back full circle to the advantages of inaction. Do nothing until events (which no one can predict) compel you to act. The apprehension that used to be expressed about the threat of reprisals by Lagos or the OAU has receded since the African governments themselves have no wish to engage in trade embargoes or sanctions. They need all the help they can get from an inhospitable world. 'Eats not morals': the message of the Threepenny Opera has arrived in the world of the 1980s.[45]

And suppose, after all, the unexpected did happen, and a revolution of black power throughout the main urban centres overwhelmed the state in an extraordinary turmoil? What price would the West have to pay if an African government seized control in Pretoria? It would depend on the extent of dislocation but, assuming that the economy was put together again in reasonable form, a future South African regime, however radical, would still need to sell its minerals and agricultural produce in Western markets, just as Marxist Angola continues to sell oil from Cabinda (via Gulf Oil) to capitalist Europe and America. A post-revolutionary Azania would hardly be less reliant, and indeed might from necessity be more dependent, on foreign earnings and Western consumers. The simple rule therefore is, wait for the market to be re-established, and offer fair terms to the new rulers.

There are also strategic interests. They are nothing like as important as they were in the 1950s and 1960s — Star Wars are globally not regionally located — but there are those who are concerned about the South Atlantic and Indian Oceans. They are not doom-eager militarists but strategists who point out that the need in 1985, from a Western standpoint, is still to ensure that the sea routes around the Cape are not controlled by a hostile — that is, pro-Soviet — regime. In that limited sense, although no one wants Mr Botha as an ally, he fits the bill.

All these different factors combine in favour of doing nothing. What is to be said on the other side? More than one might suppose, if only because the international habit of treating South Africa as a special case raises awkward issues for those who have most to do with the Republic. There is in fact a dilemma about doing nothing, despite the arguments advanced in its favour. It is a moral dilemma rather than a political, or economic, or strategic dilemma. On the one hand, the West accepts the need to recognize the sovereignty of the state as the basis of an international order regulated by diplomacy, war and the balance of power. It is, after all, largely a Western construct. South Africa is a sovereign state, it is not at war and it is part of the diplomatic world not only of the West but, increasingly, of southern Africa as a whole. On the other hand, Western politicians are also moralists. They condemn aggression as illegal, and regard breaches of human rights as an affront to the ideals by which they claim to govern. And South Africa offends. It offends in practice and in theory; the state denies the equality of its own citizens. The West cannot therefore but condemn apartheid. Hence the charge, joyfully brought by its critics, of hypocrisy: 'You help diplomatically and financially what you condemn politically and morally.'

What should be done? A simple response is to repeat what was said earlier. 'Since we trade with the Soviet Union, whose policies we oppose, since we also trade with Chile, whose record on human rights we deplore, and since we give help abroad wherever possible, as in Ethiopia, where even famine relief helps sustain an oppressive regime whose official stance is anti-Western, why should we not trade with South Africa and condemn its policies?'

Why not indeed? The case for doing so is not all hypocrisy. The difficulties, however, were too easily glossed over earlier. South Africa is still, by descent, part of a Western world of European provenance, however ugly a member of the family it has proved to be. It is also tied closely to the financial and trading interests of the Western world, however grotesque the labour base. We have to add to the relationship a further burden on the United Kingdom. Its links with the Republic are shaped as much by kinship as by policy. Of the four and a half million whites, some 40 per cent are commonly described as English-speaking (that is, not Afrikaners) and, of these, several hundred thousand are British. They hold British passports and, if trouble came, are certain to turn to London for help.

If the gulf between Western utterances of belief in democratic rights and a practical concern for market interests is uncomfortably wide, the attempt to bridge the gap has been unspectacular. The effect of ambivalence, a kindlier word than hypocrisy, can be seen in such statements as this:

The United Kingdom, like other Western countries, depends on South Africa for certain minerals important to its steel, chemical and aerospace industries. The Cape route is of economic and potentially of strategic importance. Against this background, the United Kingdom has a very real interest in encouraging peaceful change in South Africa both for its own sake and to safeguard British and wider Western interests there. In HMG's view, the resolution of the problems of South Africa and the longer-term prospects for the whole area depend on an internationally recognized settlement in Namibia and on progress within South Africa towards a form of government based on the consent of the South African people as a whole.[46]

What encouragement is intended? In practice, not very much, although some mild pressure has been applied. There is an embargo (under UN resolutions) on arms sales to and, more recently, arms purchases from South Africa. There is a Commonwealth boycott of sporting fixtures under the Gleneagles Agreement. The EEC and the United States have issued codes of practice for overseas subsidiaries within the Republic covering rates of pay, training programmes and

conditions of employment for African labour. A campaign for disinvest-
ment has been mounted in many parts of the United States, and the
Anti-Apartheid Movement mobilizes opinion in Western countries. The
effect is to add a small element of moral dignity to Western policies,
but of course it is heavily offset by the substantial returns on trade and
investment.

The dilemma may not be so awkward as to be intolerable – few
states can square their morality with their interests – but it does give
rise to the obvious question whether in fact Western governments can,
and should, do more to try to induce South Africa to change. Opinion
polls have shown a surprising willingness among the white electorate in
the Republic to endorse reform. A recent sample showed that 40 per
cent of white voters actually favoured some kind of dialogue between
the government and the ANC. Mr Botha, too, talks repeatedly of the
need to concede black political rights. Why not urge him to make good
his word? The United States and Britain veto demands at the UN for
full economic sanctions and do what they can to bring forward a settlement on Namibia by way of constructive engagement. Despite particular
quarrels, as over the Durban consulate refugees, they are the only
defenders Mr Botha is likely to find. Why not use the leverage they have
to give public support to those, like Bishop Desmond Tutu, who call on
the South African government to initiate specific reforms? It is easy to
list what they should be. Politically, talk to the ANC and the UDF.
Socially, repeal the Group Areas Act. Economically, get rid of restrictive
pass-law measures. Morally, release Nelson Mandela and his colleagues.
Legally, abolish imprisonment without trial.

It is a list of five practical reforms that would undoubtedly put an
end to 'hurtful apartheid'. Would it truly be interference for Western
governments to give them public support? Mr Harold Macmillan was
bold enough to call openly for change in 1960: could not President
Reagan and Mrs Thatcher be a little more explicit a quarter of a century
later? The hope would be to edge South Africa towards a less repressive
society in which differences of status, power and wealth would no
longer be enforced by law, a society in which all South Africans would
be citizens of a single state bound by a common patriotism.

Would such action by Western governments have any effect? The
likelihood that the West would go further than that is nil. The cost of

punitive measures, however defined, are still seen to be much higher than the embarrassment of inaction. And so long as policies are limited to persuasion, one must be sceptical of their success, though that does not mean they should not be tried. The power to nag is not altogether negligible. The hope of reform is based on the assumption that South Africa is able to change to such a degree as to shift power away from the European minority. It is founded on the belief that a sufficient number of whites will come to see that a shift in resources to non-whites will actually open up opportunities for all races within an enlarged, more prosperous economy. And because the present ideology stifles economic growth, that too may be jettisoned. Europeans would then respect non-white demands; Africans would remain loyal to an ANC commitment to non-violence. Moreover, since South Africa needs to take advantage of any upturn in the world economy, desperation may force recognition of the mutual dependence of all races. And yet the writer is very doubtful, for reasons set out in Chapter 2, whether there are grounds for such a belief. The past is too much the enemy of the future. The very nature of white society – its privileges, number, wealth, history, prejudices and short-term interests, together with a Calvinist element of self-righteousness among National Party leaders – predisposes it to hold fast to existing structures of control. Even the limited parliamentary system – the one-in-four democracy of European rule – works against major reforms: the leaders are apprehensive of the fear of their followers.

One must also note that Africans, too, are unable to escape from their past. They may begin to take a larger share of the wealth of the country today because of their greater number, and a minority among them may have more to lose in the 1980s than in the 1960s. But the evidence assembled in Chapter 2 offers no ground for believing that the millions of black South Africans will accept their inferior position, or break from attitudes of defiance established over many years. There is a consistency to their history too: it is one of mass protest and would-be rebellion, beaten back by force. Nothing in the past twenty-five years points in any other direction but that of further protest, whether it is the ANC, PAC, Black Consciousness, the UDF, the Azanian People's Organization, or similar movements in the making. Outside the national states, there are no leaders of any stature – neither Desmond Tutu of

69

the Anglican Church, nor Nthato Motlana of Soweto, nor Nelson Mandela in his prison cell — who are prepared to accept less than equality under the law and an equitable share of the resources of the state.

When one looks at South Africa today, the only plausible assumption is this: if revolution is averted, it will be because repression — not reform — is successful; if it is not averted, it will be because of the failure of repression.

The record of these pages shows that repression accompanied even the limited reforms introduced. Supported by its majority among the white electorate, the leaders of the National Party have not been afraid to coerce. Although separated by factions — Cape against the Transvaal, *verligte* against *verkrampte*, business interests against party bureaucrats — they do not disagree about the need for self-preservation. They govern by dividing their opponents while maintaining the basic features of a rigidly managed society. Can they continue to do so? It is the problem raised at the very beginning, posing the question for Britain and the West of priorities: to act or not to act. A large part of the case for not doing very much about South Africa rests (as we have seen) on the belief not only that little can be done, but that it need not be attempted; that the National Party can hold a line of control over the next ten or fifteen years; that, however disturbing the situation may be, it is not yet a source of international instability or economic disruption; that repression is effective, and the world too dangerous, too divided, too brutal for South Africa to be exceptional. How does the case stand now in the full light of inquiry?

The picture drawn in this essay does not lead the writer to be over-confident about such beliefs. Between 1984 and the end of the century many of the factors now threatening conflict will become worse. The pressure of economic forces on political structures will be stronger. The demographic balance will be more adverse — some 5.5 million whites, 3.6 million coloureds, 1 million Asians and somewhere around 35 million Africans. A radical black working-class, increasing in numbers, will be more militant. One cannot foresee what new forms of control may be enforced by the state or what the tyrannies of the twenty-first century will be able to achieve; but, equally, no certainty can be had that the violence which claws at South African society will diminish.

If an interim opinion were required, the writer would hesitantly conclude, first, that repression (not reform) will succeed in holding the line against violence for the immediate future; and, second, that disruption within the main townships will persist and cannot be ended. The economy will continue to demand new skills, the government will still impose its authority, and the dilemma of liberalization versus control will remain. Almost certainly, South Africa will become nastier, but since the armed forces and police are unlikely to be disaffected, since substantial numbers of the European electorate give every intention of supporting government policy, and since the violence that erupts is still contained within the black urban centres, one must assume that National Party rule will continue. Such conclusions, however, are no more than inferences based on personal judgment. They are not indisputable. There is no agreed prognosis and never likely to be one. The seismograph that can measure the scale of political unrest, or the barometer that can forecast changes in social pressure, is yet to be invented.

If against the odds repression does fail, then much else will fail. That one can be sure about. Down will come the whole edifice of domestic order and regional power. It will not be Brazil but Iran, and the aftermath will be grim — hunger, violence, destruction and killing. No doubt the industrial/mining base of the economy would be re-established eventually if only because the West could not allow its largest source of mineral wealth to disappear. But in spite of what we said earlier about the advantages of wait and see, the immediate damage to Western economies — resulting from the cessation of trade, the loss of investment income, the scarcity of mining supplies and the cost of substitutes — would be substantial. Britain would certainly be drawn into the crisis, along with Western Europe, the United States, the Soviet Union, the United Nations, the OAU and the poorer victims of the region. A collapsed South African state might require international rescue over a long period of recovery, and how that might be done it is impossible to foresee.

At the end of 1984 — the period that is described in this essay — the situation in the Republic, though changing, showed two constant features: an unalterable belief among National Party leaders in the need for European control, and a refusal by Africans to accept such a premise as the basis of reform. It was that fundamental antagonism which filled one with dismay. The government had imposed its authority abroad but had failed to end violence at home; the townships were in uproar and showed no signs of accepting a framework of state control. And still there was no clear idea of what should be the basis of the state, or the values of political society in the peculiar conditions of South Africa, only a clutching at notions drawn from whatever source the government believed would help it to survive. It was a melancholy picture. No intelligent observer could look at the persistent unrest in the cities, the futility of politics in the national states, the extreme poverty of many black South Africans, and the government's use of state power, without a sense of foreboding. South Africa in 1984 was full of misery and mismanagement.

Notes

1 See F. A. Hayek, *The Road to Serfdom*, ch. 10, 'Why the Worst Get to the Top' (London: Routledge & Kegan Paul, 1944).

2 Trotsky's phrase: 'From being a patriotic myth, the Russian people became an awful reality.' Africans in South Africa are currently denied even the myth of patriotism.

3 The South African Department of Statistics (Pretoria, 1984) gives the following figures for where blacks live:

(i) *White South Africa*: 11,284,173

(ii) *National states*: 11,423,942, of which:

(iii) *Self-governing homelands*		(iv) *Independent states*	
Kwazulu	3,692,000	Transkei	2,502,000
Lebowa	1,684,000	Bophuthatswana	1,425,000
KwaNdebele	162,262	Venda	339,808
Qwaqwa	169,500	Ciskei	720,807
KaNgwane	173,963		
Gazankulu	554,602		

4 A. J. Koornhof, *Soweto* (unpublished thesis, Oxford, 1984).

5 South African Breweries has now diversified and holds about 15 per cent of the national retail market in furniture, footwear, textiles and accessories. Quotations from *The Financial Times* (London), 2 October 1984.

6 *Financial Mail* (RSA), 13 January 1984.

7 A clear account of the misery caused by such clearances is given in *The Observer* (London), 6 January 1985.

8 See Hermann Giliomee and Lawrence Schlemmer, *Up Against the Fences: Poverty, Passes and Privileges in South Africa* (New Haven: Yale University Press, 1984), and the interesting history by Nigel Mandy, *A City Divided, Johannesburg and Soweto* (London: Macmillan, 1984): 'The most pressing need is to eliminate the irrational partitions which divide the city of Johannesburg against itself.'

9 14 September 1984.

10 See section B, 'The labour market', in this chapter.

11 The Tomlinson Commission had argued for a massive investment in the Bantustans in order to create 50,000 jobs per annum and thus reverse the outward flow of labour. The estimated cost was R104.5 million over an initial ten-year period. Verwoerd pared the sum

down to R36.6 million, part of which was to be raised from African taxation. The likelihood of success even at the original cost was always doubtful. The present position has been stated clearly: 'The largest part of the continuously absent Black labour force is, for all practical purposes, inseparably involved with the economy in the RSA' (*Yearbook 1984*, p. 249).

12 *Ibid.*, p. 205.

13 See n. 7 above.

14 Sam C. Nolutshungu, *Changing South Africa* (Manchester University Press, 1982), p. 89.

15 A Development Bank of South Africa was brought together in June 1983, and has tried to stimulate development in the national states. It has been a powerful instrument of persuasion in the hands of the South African government.

16 An interesting account of the quarrel between the Transkei and South Africa is given in Roger Southall, *South Africa's Transkei*, ch. 8 (London: Heinemann, 1982).

17 See Arnt Spandau, *Southern Africa and the Western World* (Reutlingen: Verlag Harwalik KG, 1984), p. 11.

18 '... the mere fact that certain abuses have been remedied draws attention to others and they now appear more galling: people may suffer less but their sensibility is exacerbated.'

19 The last two elections of the white electorate ran as follows:

	1977		1981	
Party	Seats		Seats	Votes
NP	134		131	778,371
PFP	17		26	265,297
NRP	10		8	93,603
HNP	–		–	191,249
SAP	3		–	–

Note: NRP – New Republic Party, heirs of Smuts's United Party, now largely based in Natal and crippled by defections to the NP. HNP – Herstigte Nasional Party, an 'Afrikaner-first' party led by Albert Hertzog, son of the former prime minister. SAP – South Africa Party, a right-wing splinter group. When Treurnicht resigned, Mr S.P. Botha (minister for transport) challenged him to fight a by-election. Both did so, and were joined by Mr Langley, a fellow dissident. Botha (NP) defeated Langley (CP) with a reduced majority; Treurnicht was re-elected with an increased majority. Recent by-elections have tended to confirm the trend to the CP.

20 D.F. Malan 1948–54, J.G. Strydom 1954–58, H.F. Verwoerd 1958–66, B.J. Vorster 1966–78, P.W. Botha 1978–. Before the war General Hertzog was prime minister 1924–39, followed by General Smuts 1939–48. The Afrikaner community has never cared for the turn and turn-about in office of opposed parties. Vorster became president in 1978, but resigned the following year when his

information minister, Dr Mulder, was involved in a financial scandal (see the *Report of the Erasmus Commission*).

21 Coloured families can still drive past the new flats and bungalows of District Six that was once their traditional quarter in Cape Town before it was flattened to make room for a new white suburb. Similarly, Mr Pen Cotze (minister of community development until 1984) was contemptuously dismissive of Indians living in the white suburb of Mayfair in Johannesburg — living there in contravention of the Group Areas Act, not out of choice but out of necessity because of the housing waiting-list of over 10,000 applicants for their own quarter. 'These people didn't live in the sky before they came to Mayfair. They can go back to where they came from.' That in the month prior to the 1984 elections.

22 'His passage booked to Bombay, Gandhi sat down to a farewell dinner organized by Dada Abdulla. At the table he picked up a newspaper and saw the headline: "Indian Franchise Bill". The legislature of Natal was hastening to use its newly-acquired powers of self-government to restrict the number of the self-governed by taking the vote away from the Indians. Gandhi turned the dinner into a political meeting . . . and founded the Natal Indian Congress.' The date was 1894. George Woodcock, *Gandhi* (London: Fontana/ Collins, 1972), p. 33.

23 The issue was troublesome not only for the six and for the British government but for Rajbansi and Hendrickse. Although members now of the government, they were not consulted about the detention orders. The government argued that since they were ministers without portfolio they had no responsibility under the new constitution.

24 *Commission of Inquiry into Legislation Affecting the Utilization of Manpower* (Pretoria, 1979), Chairman P.J. Riekert. *Commission of Inquiry into Labour Legislation* (Pretoria, Parts 1, 2, 3, 4, 1979–80), Chairman N.E. Wiehahn.

25 'The very unequal price of labour which we frequently find in places at no great distance from one another is owing to the obstruction which the law gives to the poor man who would carry his labour from one area to another without a certificate.' The passage might almost be a paraphrase of criticism submitted to Professor Wiehahn and Dr Riekert. It is actually Adam Smith, writing against the effect on the mobility of labour of the poor law, which, two centuries ago, he saw as 'evident violation of liberty'.

26 Preliminary findings from the two-year survey were submitted to a conference in Cape Town in April 1984. Quotations are from the summaries of papers, *Lincoln Letter*, July 1984 (published by the Lincoln Trust, London); emphasis in the original.

27 Koornhof, *Soweto*, pp. 396–7.

28 Leonard Thompson, 'South Africa and Decolonization', in Prosser Gifford and Roger Louis (eds), *The Transfer of Power in Africa*

(New Haven: Yale University Press, 1982), p. 444. See, too, Heribert Adam and Hermann Giliomee, *Ethnic Power Mobilized: Can South Africa Change?* (New Haven: Yale UP, 1979), and Leonard Thompson and Andrew Prior, *South African Politics* (New Haven: Yale UP, 1982).

29 A summary of the riots can be found in Reina R. Steenwijk, *Unrest in Black Townships in the Transvaal* (Amsterdam, December 1984). For the behaviour of the police, see *Police Conduct during Township Protests August–November 1984* (London: Catholic Institute for International Relations, 1984).

30 Section 28 permits indefinite preventive detention without trial. Section 29 allows indefinite detention for interrogation of those deemed to be a threat to law and order. Both Chris Dhlamini of the Federation of South African Trade Unions (FOSATU) and Phiroshaw Camay of the Council of Unions of South Africa (CUSA) were detained without charge or trial.

31 Figures taken from *Lincoln Letter*, July 1984.

32 See Charles Simkins, 'Can the State Achieve Educational Equality?', *Die Suid Afrikaan*, Spring 1984. Mr Simkins calculated expenditure on different projections to the year 2000 for low, medium and high growth in the economy, and correlated them with small, medium and large welfare budgets (i.e. scales of generosity). His conclusions were: 'In the case of the small welfare budget and slow growth, per capita expenditure would actually be lower on average in 2000 than it was in 1975/6. Whatever the growth outcome, the average would be lower than the 1975/6 level enjoyed by Asians. In the case of the medium welfare budget and the medium growth projection, the per capita expenditure in the year 2000 would be the same as received by coloureds and Asians in 1975/6. In other words, if the equalization of per capita expenditure were achieved by 2000, everyone would enjoy the same level of services as coloureds and Asians had enjoyed a quarter of a century earlier, given the realization of the most probable projections. Even in the 'high-high case', equalization would mean standards dropping 28 per cent for whites, though rising for everyone else.' The article was a condensed form of a paper (No. 253) submitted to the Carnegie Conference on Poverty, University of Cape Town, April 1984.

33 *Star* (Johannesburg), 3 October 1984.

34 The following account, headed 'The Case of the 76 Squatters', is from *Black Sash Report* (1984):

'Lodgers from overcrowded township houses made a stand to provide their own housing on a piece of vacant land. They were joined by groups of people, some of them "illegals", who had been squatting in the bushes around the three main townships. The spiral of demolitions, arrests and returns to the site began.

'After a night of drama — with the police rolling barbed wire around the chanting people in the camp, flooding the area with arc lights and throwing tear-gas canisters — all the "illegals" who had not run away were arrested and all the "legals" were moved into two empty beer halls.

'Bail applications on behalf of those arrested were rejected and the group of 76 squatters were held in custody until their cases were heard.

'Attorneys, appearing *pro amico*, did everything in their power to show that these people had no alternative but to come to Cape Town to look for work. The drought, the economic conditions in Transkei and Ciskei and the devastation of settled family life by the migrant labour system were all put forward in the defence arguments. To no avail. The magistrate expressed his sympathy but found them guilty of illegal squatting and being in the area without permission. He sentenced them/to R50 or 50 days on each count, suspended on condition that they left the area immediately.

'Many of these "illegal" people simply moved further into the bush or to Crossroads. By the end of the year Crossroads was being raided on numerous occasions and all structures repeatedly demolished. Eventually arrests were made and those without previous convictions (a total of 35) were found guilty on the squatting charge and sentenced/to R90 or 90 days, suspended for three years on condition that they leave the area immediately. The remaining 13 had their previously suspended sentences enforced and were sent to prison for five months without the option of a fine.

'The people put in the beer halls were destined to be moved to Khayelitsha — a township being hastily constructed in the sand dunes. Khayelitsha means "new home".'

35 A good account can be found in *Overview: Southern African Development Coordination Conference* (London: Catholic Institute for International Relations, January 1985). SADCC was formed in April 1980 by nine nations: the five former 'front-line states' — Zambia, Tanzania, Angola, Mozambique and Botswana — plus Zimbabwe, Malawi, Swaziland and Lesotho. Emphasis is given to rail communications, food production, energy resources and training.

36 See Gerhard Erasmus, *The Accord of Nkomati: Context and Content* (Johannesburg: South African Institute of International Affairs, October 1984): 'It would be misleading to create the impression that South Africa was in an unassailable position . . . South Africa's military expenditure has become extremely expensive. Campaigns such as Operation Askari in Angola add to this expense. The SADF encountered sophisticated Soviet weaponry for which they were not fully prepared. To become so would necessitate a further round of arms development that South Africa can ill afford . . .'

37 See Reina R. Steenwijk, *The Ingwavuma/Kangwane Land Deal* (Amsterdam: Information Centre on South Africa, 1982), from which the quotations are taken.

38 *Financial Mail* 23 March 1984.

39 Speech to the Royal Commonwealth Society, 25 July 1984

(privately circulated).

40 *Financial Mail*, 23 March 1984.

41 'It may be inferred from meetings between Lt-Gen. Van der Westhuizen, head of South Africa's military security, and the Zimbabwean security minister, Emmerson Munangagwa, that some understanding exists between the two countries about Super-Zapu infiltration through Botswana from South Africa.' 'South Africa in the 1980s', *Update* (London), no. 2, December 1984.

42 A good, detailed account is given in Michael Spicer, 'The Lusaka Talks and Prospects for Namibian Independence', *Background Briefing*, no. 17 (Johannesburg: South African Institute of International Affairs, 1983).

43 Spandau, *Southern Africa and the Western World*, p.10.

44 See James Barber, Jesmond Blumenfeld and Christopher R. Hill, *The West and South Africa*, Chatham House Papers, no. 14 (London: Routledge & Kegan Paul, for R11A, 1982), particularly Part 2, Jesmond Blumenfeld, 'Economic Relations and Political Leverage', in which the case against sanctions is argued very cogently.

45 Bertolt Brecht, 'Erst Kommt das Fressen, dann Kommt die Moral', *Die Dreigroschenoper*, finale.

46 Great Britain, House of Commons, Foreign Affairs Committee, *Minutes of Evidence*, 13 May 1981.

Index

Index

2 pm
Thuis
14 Nov

Book of the Day

Routledge & Kegan Paul PLC

14 LEICESTER SQUARE, LONDON WC2H 7PH

TELEPHONE: 01 437 9011

TELEX: 262941 RKP G

The Publishers present their compliments to the Editor and have pleasure in sending for review a copy of the accompanying publication. They would greatly appreciate receiving a marked copy of the journal containing any notice that may be given to the book.

N.B. Reviews should not appear in the press prior to the date of publication.

South Africa 1984
Chatham House Paper No. 26
Dennis Austin

ISBN 0 7102 0620 8

Published Price £5.95

Date of Publication 27th June 1985